To Mum & Dad
Shirley & Weldon Coleman

Marco Island, Florida's Gulf Playground
Michael Coleman

Book Design:
Janice Davidson, www.janicedavidsondesign.com

Front & Back Cover Images:
Majestic aerial of Marco Island & Marco sunset by Barry Howe

Media Partners:
Marco Island Sun Times, www.marcoislandflorida.com
The Marco Review, www.marcoreview.com

Library of Congress Control Number: 2014905590
ISBN 978-1-4951-0630-9

First Edition

Published by Marco Island Ink
www.marcoislandbook.com
marcohistory@hotmail.com

Printed in U.S.A.

Marco Island

FLORIDA'S GULF PLAYGROUND

BY MICHAEL COLEMAN

TABLE OF CONTENTS

FOREWARD

There's more to Marco Island than meets the eye.

Much more.

This special place first captivated me in 1931. I was just 12 years old but driving over from Miami with my father to fish and swim here and to learn of its secret past was pure magic.

Long before Marco Island became a sun, beach, shelling, golf, boating and fishing haven, explorer Juan Ponce de Leon's fountain of youth may very well have been located here. Local legend also tells of a centuries-old native Indian curse plus buried gold treasure worth millions of dollars just a few feet below the surface of our majestic crescent-shaped beach.

Magic, indeed.

BIG DREAMS

Soon, larger-than-life dreamers, some with enormous personal wealth, would arrive in an attempt to tame Marco. Few ever did. The Marco Island story is and has always been about failure and resiliency, triumph and, sadly, unspeakable tragedy.

The modern era, too, has had its fair share of novel-like twists and turns en route to a remarkable maturation process. We owe it all to three brothers – my bosses – Deltona Corporation executives Elliott, Robert and Frank Mackle Jr. who, long before guidebooks, websites and apps became the norm, sized up the island's potential in the early 1960s and against all odds built the most unique resort/leisure community in U.S. history.

The stories you are about to experience in *Marco Island, Florida's Gulf Playground*, crafted by the best authors, writers and photographers this island has ever produced, could not be more enticing.

Two-time Marco Island history book author Michael Coleman and his editorial team have explored it all, seamlessly capturing the essence of Marco Island in each amazing era. The compelling editorial narrative, coupled with dozens of inspiring images, chronicles life here like it has never been chronicled before.

MESMERIZING EVENTS

It's almost impossible to fathom all that has occurred here over the centuries, given the island's small geographic size and remote location, but Coleman's take on our recent history is mesmerizing to say the least.

- Observe how the Mackle brothers built today's playground from scratch yet lost a fortune in the process.

- Gasp at a kidnapping that shocked the nation.

- Be inspired by our tie to man's first moon walk.

- Decide for yourself if Marco was a vital CIA eavesdropping post at the height of the Cold War.

- Learn about a sports tragedy that resulted in Marco Island hosting "the greatest one-day golf tournament in America" for over a decade.

- Shake your head in disbelief because the first woman named to the FBI's 10 Most Wanted list actually had a connection here.

- Celebrate with us as we bask in the glow of being named TripAdvisor's No. 1 island travel destination in America and fourth best in the world.

Meanwhile, further back in the annals of island history, Coleman has also uncovered equally impressive gems.

LEFT: MARCO ISLAND TODAY AND MARCO ISLAND, 1964

TOP: THE MACKLE BROTHERS; JACK NICKLAUS AND BOB HOPE ON MARCO

Did you know:

- An archaeological dig unearthed artifacts so historically significant that they are housed at the Smithsonian Institution?

- The first island hotel charged visitors $1 a night and it featured a two-story outhouse?

- Prolific clam factories employed men, women *and* children here and that a railway went bust after clam stocks declined?

- A major horse racing track, where towering condominiums now stand, would have been operational next to a bustling deep water sea port without equal?

THE MAGIC LIVES ON

On the pages that follow, relive the joys, challenges and heartache of those who came before us and be awed by the one constant: Nature at her best. Plus, learn the names of a golf icon, New York Yankee great, and heavyweight boxing champion of the world who each called Marco Island home.

In *Marco Island, Florida's Gulf Playground*, Coleman brings these and many other fascinating stories about our rich history to life.

What a pleasure to relive all of Marco Island's unique magic — the good, bad, past and present — in this one-of-a-kind book.

Enjoy!

Herbert Rosser Savage, Architect

(No one has better personified the hope and optimism of modern Marco Island than 95-year-old Savage, a tireless champion here since 1965. He designed Marco Island's first homes, the Marco Beach Hotel (today's Marriott), and scores of other island buildings. He resides on Marco with his wife Emily . . . Michael Coleman).

LEFT: BURNHAM CLAM FACTORY WORKERS; WORLD CHAMPION SAND SCULPTING ARTISTS JOHN & LAURA GOWDY AT MARRIOTT; A HERON ON THE BEACH

NEXT PAGE: CAPE MARCO

A NOTE FROM THE AUTHOR

Alluring Marco Island has been capturing hearts, minds and souls for centuries.

With its sub-tropical climate, Ten Thousand uninhabited neighboring islands and the awe-inspiring Everglades at her doorstep, life here is pure nirvana for the close to 17,000 full-time residents who call it home. Some 40,000 enjoy the spoils "in season."

Beyond the endless sunshine, beaches, recreational pursuits and glowing visitor testimonials, you might be surprised to learn that epic Shakespearean tragedy has occurred here in virtually every era. But with each passing decade, like the coming and going of her gentle Gulf of Mexico tides, Marco Island has evolved into the world-class resort/leisure community it was destined to become.

WE'RE NO. 1

Among a host of recent accolades, Marco was ranked the No. 1 island in the U.S. and fourth best in the world by TripAdvisor in 2014. The world's largest on-line travel site declared Marco the "perfect destination for those who crave a peaceful retreat." Additionally, a *National Geographic* book recently showcased the local Ten Thousand Island's Dolphin Project, declaring it and the island to be among the top 100 places on the planet that can change a child's life.

LEFT: MARCO'S MAJESTIC BEACH, 1967 AND TODAY

THE MACKLE BROTHERS, ELLIOTT, ROBERT AND FRANK JR.

The Marco Island story is about entrepreneurs, many ahead of their time, and an archaeological dig of historic proportions that brought global attention to the island for the first time. It's about three developers — Deltona Corporation executives Elliott, Robert and Frank Mackle Jr. — who carved today's paradise from an alligator-infested swamp. It's about beautiful, multimillion-dollar homes on man-made canals and sportsmen the world over either fishing in her waters or heading out on her links.

The Marco Island story is also about tourism.

W.D. Capt. Bill Collier, the son of the island's founder, built the glorious Marco Hotel at the turn of the 20th century despite the fact Marco's geographic location could not have been more remote. The Olde Marco Inn, as it is named today, still stands as a precursor to the three gleaming, world-class resorts that overlook the Gulf of Mexico. Marriott, Hilton and Marco Beach Ocean Resort beckon tourists from across the globe to shores graced by sunsets more radiant than anywhere on earth.

This book, which covers centuries of Marco Island history, has been 20 years in the making. Since I first collaborated with the Marco Island Area Chamber of Commerce to write *Marco Island Culture & History* in 1995 — in celebration of the modern era's 30th birthday — hardly a month has passed without someone sharing with me an island anecdote or photograph from an aging family album. Surely I would include such nuggets in a second book, if I was ever to write one. And, what was once a fledgling local historical society two decades ago is now a flourishing community resource complete with a stunning new multimillion-dollar Marco Island Historical Museum that houses an ever-growing archive and exhibit space. Maybe a second book — in celebration of modern Marco's 50th birthday in 2015 — would be in the cards after all.

I have been joined on the pages that follow by an impressive team of writers and photographers who have brought Marco Island's rich history to life. It has been a labor of love, in the truest sense, working with so many talented individuals who have been chronicling life here in various mediums for decades.

BRINGING MARCO'S PAST TO LIFE

Thank you to authors Elizabeth "Betsy" Perdichizzi, Don Farmer, Chris Curle and Tom Williams; writer/historian Marion Nicolay; *Marco Island Sun Times* journalist Quentin Roux and photographers Joel Gewirtz and Barry Howe. Each and every contributor is a permanent resident of Marco Island and we all proudly call it home.

I had the pleasure of writing about the early pioneers plus the Mackle brothers with two pros: Perdichizzi and Nicolay.

Four-time Marco Island history book author Perdichizzi was an enormous help, with an assist from her husband Bill, as we produced the pioneer narrative. Betsy will take you back to a time where local residents endured unthinkable hardship — enormous challenges, searing heat, bugs and few conveniences.

Nicolay, meanwhile, has amazed me since I met her more than two decades ago. She has written extensively about the Mackle brothers and while that may not seem to be much of a stretch for some, she has done so legally blind. Her dedicated work ethic and attention to detail on this book was both greatly appreciated and admired.

Award-winning journalist Roux, who has written more stories and taken more images of local residents than anyone in the past 20 years having worked at two of the island's three newspapers, deftly handled the post-Mackle era through present day and complemented his far-reaching editorial contribution with equally impressive photographs.

And, who better than novelists Farmer and Curle, among CNN's first anchors and for decades *Marco Island Eagle* columnists, to delve into the numerous personalities, celebrities, sports and business titans who have either visited or called Marco Island home?

Williams, an award-winning, two-time novelist, concludes this book with a fine essay. He was drawn to the island in his early 20s and for the past 35 years has navigated the seemingly endless maze of local waterways as a boat captain for Marriott. Observing the island from such a unique perch, with tantalizing sunsets concluding most of his days, he was the obvious choice to capture the essence of Marco Island. Or, as island architect Herb Savage articulated in the foreward to this book, its magic.

Gewirtz, the proud publisher of his own photography book celebrating Marco Island, kindly reviewed his immense archives for just the right images to be included in this publication and for that I am grateful.

LEFT: HILTON MARCO ISLAND BEACH RESORT AND SPA

Howe, whose aerial artistry is simply breathtaking, has taken some of the most beautiful bird's-eye photographs of cities across the nation and his work on this book, including the magnificent front and back covers, is beyond reproach.

Thanks are in order as well to the Naples, Marco Island, Everglades Convention and Visitors Bureau for their timely editorial and photographic assistance.

BAHR, SAVAGE CONTRIBUTION

Of the host of interviews conducted to create this book, no one provided more knowledge, depth or insight with regards to the development of modern Marco Island than two Deltona executives: The late sales chief Neil Bahr and Savage.

Bahr graciously took time in his retirement years to share with me the joys and deep sorrows associated with building a paradise from swamp land, before his passing in 2010. He was the last man alive from an exclusive group of five executives who innocently sized up the island's enormous potential as they stood on Marco Island's deserted beach in 1962 in awe of the sheer, undeveloped landscape before their eyes. The Mackle brothers and chief architect Jim Vensel — the four men with Bahr on the beach back then — have all passed on.

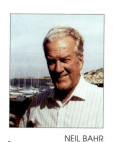

NEIL BAHR

Savage, at 95 years of age and still practising his craft, kindly wrote this book's foreward. As you learned by reading his introduction, he had a front row seat designing the modern era's first homes plus eventually, his masterpiece, the Marco Beach Hotel & Villas (now Marriott) in 1971. Island progress, however, has not been kind to Savage's many Polynesian-themed structures. "If there was an award for the most homes torn down, I would win," he once lamented as larger homes are now built on lots where Savage's originals once stood.

I am truly honored and deeply indebted having been a fly on the wall in the presence of both Bahr and Savage during a host of separate interviews over the years as they reminisced most fondly about an era not so long ago yet one now almost, it seems, light years away.

MACKLE RISE AND FALL

Marco Island is what it is today because of their bosses, the Mackle brothers, who bet the farm on mosquito-infested acreage on Florida's unproven Gulf Coast. The swamp land and twisted mangroves were hardly alluring but great men with big dreams saw a playground like no other. The brothers and their monumental undertaking have personally fascinated me for decades. A great deal of this book is devoted to their rise *and* fall.

Was the vision worth it?

KIDNAPPER'S PHOTO OF BARBARA JANE MACKLE

A Mackle daughter was kidnapped and buried alive near the height of the island's global promotional blitz in the late 1960s — the Marco buzz attracted more than just potential new home owners — and, despite the gleam of today's beach front condominiums and impressive homes on a series of perfectly carved man-made canals, the brothers would lose enormous personal treasure along the way to keep the dream alive.

What could possibly have fueled their demise?

The saga has been revealed on these pages thanks to the candor of Bahr, Savage and the always amenable Frank Mackle III, who worked side-by-side with his father and uncles as a top-ranking Deltona executive in his own right. Frank III could not have been kinder or more generous with his time to assist me and the other writers contributing to this project. Thank you, Mr. Mackle.

A HELPING HAND

Books like this don't get off the ground without a good story to tell and certainly not without backers who believe in it. While I am grateful to the writers and photographers plus island residents who were interviewed over the years to create this publication — many of whom have since passed on — I am most deeply indebted to Rich Masterson, General Manager, and Joe Taylor, Editor, of the *Marco Island Sun Times* (a Gannett Company) who kindly partnered with me on this project. You'll notice there is no advertising in this publication. My desire from the outset was to purely showcase the integrity of the island's history but had it not been for the weekly promotion of this book in the *Sun Times*, in print and online, the far-and-wide reach I had hoped for would not have remotely occurred.

My other media partner, *The Marco Review*, was equally pivotal. The island's favorite visitor guide for over 20 years, publishers Stephen and Debbie Barker and their team also provided key in print and online space to promote the book you now hold.

Thanks are also in order to the following: the incredibly talented Janice Davidson who designed this book — it's as impressive as the history it contains; Austin Bell, Curator of Collections, Marco Island Historical Society for kindly granting me access to their archives; Rick Medwedeff, General Manager, Michael Tighe, Resident Manager, Robert Pfeffer, Director of Sales & Marketing, Susan Ryziw, Executive Assistant and Cathy Nelson, Executive Assistant, Marco Island Marriott Beach Resort Golf Club & Spa; Mac Chaudhry, General Manager, Hilton Marco Island Beach Resort and Spa; Paul Ditheridge, Vice President, Marketing and Sales and Lessly Trejo, Marketing Assistant, Olshan Properties (Hilton Marco Island Beach Resort and Spa); Ana Kusmider, Marketing Manager, Marco Beach Ocean Resort; Sandi Riedemann Lazarus, Executive Director, Marco Island Area Chamber of Commerce; JoNell Modys, Public Relations and Communications Manager, Naples, Marco Island, Everglades Convention and Visitors Bureau; Mark Bahr, owner/operator, Marco Island Watersports; Patricia Berry, a key executive of the Marco Island film and soap opera festivals; and Gretchen Baldus, City of Marco Island.

Thank you, as well, to Mary Sarazen Ilnicki; local artists Peter Sottong, Ted Morris and Jo-Ann Sanborn; photographers David Hall, Gary Kufner, Steve Beaudet, Pat Shapiro and Peter Berec; realtors Kathy Hunt and Chris Costin Sullivan; the Barron Collier Companies; officials at the Collier County Museum and State of Florida archives; and Steve MacLeod, whose timely edits were greatly appreciated.

marcoislandflorida.com

Marco Island's BEST Visitor Magazine.... It's ALL you need!

DECADES-LONG HOARDING

Finally, my first book would not have been published, or this one, without the generosity of the late Leonard Llewellyn, a former Navy/Marine Corps Top Gun and Air Force One pilot to presidents John F. Kennedy and Lyndon B. Johnson. Llewellyn would later move on to become one of Deltona's top Marco Island sales leaders — year in and year out — before going it alone to launch his own real estate company on the island.

When I started interviewing older residents and began poking around libraries and newspaper archives for my first book 20 years ago, stories about Marco Island abounded. However, photographs of Marco Island, especially during the early development of the modern era where the magnificent beach lay deserted and bulldozers carved the first streets and waterfront canals, were virtually non existent. How could I possibly write a hardcover coffee table book without any images?

Llewellyn caught wind of my quandary and, over a beer or two at a local watering hole in 1995, he cautiously sized up my intent. Days later, he invited me to his office where he produced a treasure trove of dust-covered files and those coveted photographs, many of which had never been published let alone seen the light of day in decades. He also handed me photographs of many of the early pioneers — images that did not exist in any local library or archive to that point.

I was a kid in a candy store. Other than Frank Mackle III, who has since meticulously written an online history about his father and uncles, I had not seen anything like it. I shudder to think what would have become of those files and photographs had Llewellyn not been such a magnificent, decades-long hoarder. He passed away in 2010.

I am delighted, and I hope you are too, that Llewellyn's monumental gift — accompanied this time by an expanded editorial and photographic narrative — lives on.

Michael Coleman

LEONARD LLEWELLYN

EIGHT OF MARCO ISLAND'S TOP WRITERS AND PHOTOGRAPHERS COLLABORATED WITH AUTHOR MICHAEL COLEMAN TO PUBLISH *MARCO ISLAND, FLORIDA'S GULF PLAYGROUND* IN CELEBRATION OF THE MODERN ERA'S 50TH BIRTHDAY IN 2015. BACK ROW, FROM LEFT, MARION NICOLAY, DON FARMER, CHRIS CURLE, ELIZABETH "BETSY" PERDICHIZZI; MIDDLE ROW, BARRY HOWE, QUENTIN ROUX, JOEL GEWIRTZ; SEATED, COLEMAN AND TOM WILLIAMS.

BEFORE AND AFTER:
MARCO HOTEL CIRCA 1920s AND OLDE MARCO INN TODAY

BEFORE AND AFTER: MARCO BEACH OCEAN RESORT PRIOR TO ITS 2001 OPENING, AND TODAY

BEFORE AND AFTER:
TOP LEFT, MARCO BEACH HOTEL, 1965

BELOW, MARCO BEACH HOTEL
& VILLAS, 1972

TOP RIGHT, TODAY'S MARCO
ISLAND MARRIOTT BEACH RESORT
GOLF CLUB & SPA

TODAY'S PLAYGROUND

Marco Island may very well be the planet's ultimate outdoor playground.

The largest and most northerly in a chain of Ten Thousand Islands stretching to the southern tip of the Florida mainland, modern Marco Island's unspoiled natural habitat is home to beach lovers, golfers, boaters, shellers, fishermen, kayak and canoe paddlers, photographers and more.

Marco sits within Collier County, the state's second largest land and water mass. The Isles of Capri and Goodland, nearby, plus the City of Naples, just north, and Everglades City, to the south, are the island's nearest neighbors.

The county features huge preserves which provide a haven for numerous rare and endangered animal and bird species. Flanked by some 100 miles of islands, bays and estuaries that will never be developed, Big Cypress National Preserve, Audubon Corkscrew Swamp Sanctuary, Rookery Bay National Estuarine Research Reserve, Ten Thousand Islands National Wildlife Refuge, Briggs Nature Center at Rookery Bay, Collier-Seminole State Park, Fakahatchee Strand Preserve State Park and the ubiquitous Everglades National Park provide an eco-paradise for nature enthusiasts of all ages.

The Everglades, in fact, is the only place on earth where alligators and crocodiles exist in the same habitat. Among the other wonders here, bottlenose dolphins, manatees, loggerhead turtles, sea otters, wood storks, brown and white pelicans, roseate spoonbills, herons and egrets are common sightings on a daily basis, year-round.

LEFT: MARCO ROMANCE
RIGHT: THE GULF BECKONS

LOTS TO SEE & DO

Sun seekers rejoice. Sophisticated, full-service beach front properties — Marriott, Hilton and Marco Beach Ocean Resort — are sprinkled along the island's western shore. Each offer lounge chairs, umbrellas and a host of water sport rentals from kayaks, canoes and wave runners to stand-up paddleboards, sightseeing cruises and parasailing. Some of the island's finest dining experiences can also be found at these world-class facilities.

Near the island's north end, the first of three public beach access points awaits visitors. The 32-acre Tigertail Beach Park is a great spot for beach activities and wildlife viewing. The Great Florida Birding Trail Guide lists the park as one of the best all-around birding locations in all of Southwest Florida. Park rangers offer several educational programs including birding tours and presentations on coastal wildlife (sea turtles, manatees and dolphins). The park features showers, restrooms, a large playground and a concession stand.

Public beach access also extends to a mid-island locale, its somewhat secluded entrance running parallel to the Madeira condominium on South Collier Blvd. Limited parking and no facilities. Meanwhile, farther south, with the Apollo condominium complex as your marker, South Marco Beach features public parking and restrooms but no other facilities.

Marco's majestic beaches and sand bars offer some of the finest shelling opportunities in the world. Shell seekers will be rewarded with a treasury of moon shells, angel wings, whelks, lion's paws, olive shells, scallops and hundreds of other exotic varieties

Backcountry fishing is also very popular around Marco and those enjoying time on our waters reel in plenty of snook, tarpon, redfish, trout, pompano and many other species. Experienced guides are readily available for fishing excursions and include backcountry flats fishing and deep-sea charters into the Gulf of Mexico for grouper, kingfish and snapper.

Golf enthusiasts will find links at every turn in Southwest Florida. The island itself is home to two private clubs: The steeped-in-history Island Country Club and Hideaway Beach Club. Just minutes off island, Marriott operates The Rookery at Marco and the Hammock Bay Golf & Country Club.

Marco offers many shopping treasures. Specialty shops and boutiques feature everything from bathing suits and island wear to the finest designer fashions and art work. Shopping goes beyond beach wear, with stores that offer artistic items of local flavor and interesting souvenirs.

A plethora of dining choices also awaits. Seafood is typically king for obvious reasons. Succulent Gulf shrimp year-round and seasonal stone crab claws easily top everyone's list.

Marco Island is home to a host of accommodations ranging from luxurious waterfront resorts to small motels and the iconic Olde Marco Inn, the longest-running business here having opened its doors in 1896. In addition, hundreds of private condominiums, beautiful homes and timeshares are located from the Gulf beaches to local neighborhoods.

WATER WATER EVERYWHERE

Marco Island is a paradise for boaters. In addition to being surrounded by the Marco River, the Gulf of Mexico and Barfield and Caxambas bays, it is also crisscrossed by man-made canals. The private Marco Island Yacht Club has for decades been the place to see and be seen. Meanwhile, full-service marinas offer boat rentals, transient slips and fishing charters into the nearby Ten Thousand Islands. Shelling and sightseeing cruises aboard sailboats are available for those seeking a change of pace … prepare to sit back, relax and enjoy the scenery. Among the sights: Magnificent waterside mansions, marine life and, of course, gorgeous sunsets. Many cruises include a stop on an island for shelling. For a more hands-on adventure, enjoy a guided kayak or canoe eco-tour. They, too, are readily available here.

Having enjoyed such recreational pursuits, look for plenty of casual opportunities to enhance your Marco Island experience. Throughout the year various seafood festivals and fairs bring islanders and visitors together. Farmer's Market, especially, running from November through April at Veterans Community Park, is a must, as is an exhibit tour at The Marco Island Center for the Arts or a performance at Marco Players Theater.

Learning about Marco's amazing history can be equally rewarding.

Thanks to the efforts of the Marco Island Area Chamber of Commerce, a dozen key historic markers across the island chart much of it. See where a famous 1896 archaeological dig took place and harken back to a time when men, women *and* children worked side-by-side in two prolific clam factories. A local trolley tour has it covered.

The island also has a new multimillion-dollar facility to showcase its past. The Marco Island Historical Museum, the first permanent structure built to celebrate all things Marco, opened in 2010.

It, like the stories revealed on the pages that follow, will amaze.

LEFT: BEACH BOARDWALK, TANNING BLISS
RIGHT: THE JOY OF MARCO: SHELLING AND GOLFING

NEXT SPREAD: MARCO AT HER FINEST

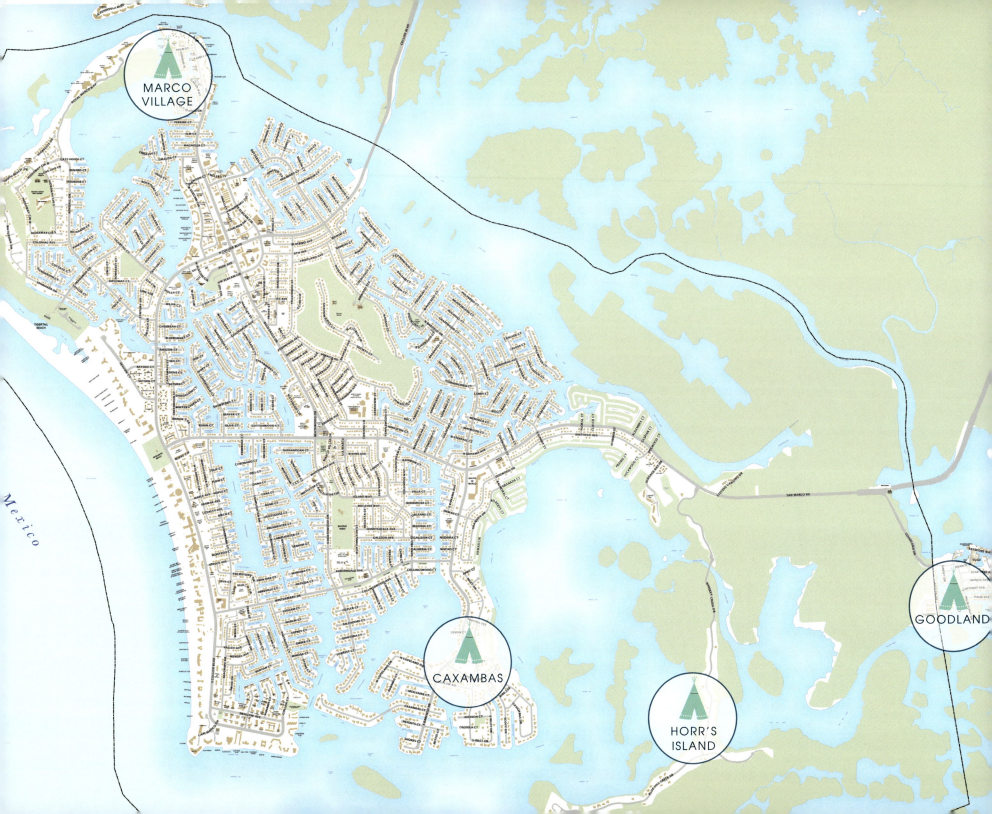

MARCO
VILLAGE

CAXAMBAS

HORR'S
ISLAND

GOODLAND

Mexico

MARCO ISLAND'S FIRST RESIDENTS

Some 5,000 years before Marco Island's multimillion-dollar waterfront houses dotted the landscape, this special place was home to ancient Indian civilizations.

By the time Christopher Columbus set sail to explore the New World, Calusa Indians were flourishing here and in neighboring regions along the lower west coast of La Florida.

As many as four locations in and around Marco Island were occupied at various times over the years by the Calusa . . . Marco village in the north (today's Olde Marco), Caxambas and Horr's Island (today's Key Marco) to the south, and in nearby Goodland to the southeast.

Researchers believe at the height of their existence some 10,000 Calusa lived on the Gulf Coast. Hundreds are said to have called Marco Island home believing it was sacred. In fact, Marco Island may very well have been the hub of religious ceremonies.

Calusa here enjoyed bountiful seafood harvests with both land and sea providing raw materials for clothing, tools and shelter. Expert woodworkers, they often carved hollowed-out canoes, beams and planks for their houses, docks and piers, and they were skilled hunters with both the spear thrower and the bow and arrow.

SHELL MOUND BUILDERS

The most intriguing aspect of Calusa life, however, may have been the ingenious use of shells in their daily lives. Instead of simply discarding them after their feasts, shells were placed on primitive building sites. As more shells were added to the mound, homes and places of worship were not just built but elevated high above any flooding from heavy rain fall.

The highest island shell mound stands some 52 feet above sea level on Indian Hill located in the present-day "Estates" section of Marco Island. It remains the highest elevated ground in all of Southwest Florida.

CALUSA INDIAN SETTLEMENTS

RIGHT: ARTIST RENDERING OF THE KEY MARCO CAT. COURTESY BERNIE ROSENBERG

A series of archeological digs over the decades has produced fine hand-carved Calusa works — masks and animal heads, for instance — that were often painted and used in artistic and religious ceremonies.

Many of the Calusa artifacts found here were first unearthed by accident when W. D. Capt. Bill Collier, the son of the island's founder, toiled in his garden. Archeologist Frank Hamilton Cushing was summoned in 1896 to Collier's home at Marco village (present-day Olde Marco at the north end of the island, although Cushing dubbed it Key Marco), where he led an excavation team funded by the Smithsonian Institution, University of Pennsylvania, and the wife of newspaper publishing baron William Randolph Hearst. The Pepper-Hearst expedition included distinguished artist/photographer Wells Sawyer.

The expedition, having garnered some 2,000 artifacts, was deemed by many scholars and academics as one of the most significant excavations in North American history.

The most prominent find was a kneeling, half-man, half-panther figurine dubbed the Key Marco Cat. Made of buttonwood and standing a mere six inches in height, it is such a revered treasure that it remains safely housed to this day at the Smithsonian Institution.

MARCO GETS ITS NAME

Some of Spain's most celebrated navigators and conquistadors, with a thirst for adventure, personal wealth and a chance to win new souls to the church, were eager to tackle the virgin shores of La Florida in the 1500s. A companion of Columbus, Juan Ponce de Leon, led the first European exploration of Florida from Puerto Rico in 1513. After rounding the Florida Keys and in search of fresh water he is believed to have made land fall in the vicinity of Caxambas, at the south end of today's Marco Island, where two cool artesian springs were located.

The Spaniards are credited with naming the island and its inhabitants. It was obviously a favorite place to fill casks with fresh water for the return trip to Spain. "Caxymbas" and later "Cabo d'Aguada" were quickly noted on maps. Thus, the name Caxambas — Indian for fresh water — is one of the oldest place names in North America. And while the name meant a life-saving stopover for sailors, the island itself became known as La Isla de San Marco (the Island of Saint Mark), named for Saint Mark, the Christian evangelist and traditional author of the second gospel in the Bible. Over the years it became known as San Marco Island (Saint Mark's Island) and eventually Marco Island. It would feature a variety of communities and interchangeable names — Malco, Maco, Marco, Key Marco, Marco village, Old Marco, Olde Marco, Caxambas, Collier City, Collier City North, Collier City South — but whatever era and the name associated with it, it would forever be known as the largest and most northerly of the Ten Thousand Islands.

The diseases that Spanish explorers and slave hunters introduced from Europe proved far deadlier against the Calusa and other Florida Indians than fire arms or cannon. Entire villages, including the dwellers in and around present-day Marco, were swept away by epidemics of small pox, measles and typhus. By the mid 1700s the once powerful Calusa had been annihilated. Historians speculate that the survivors may have joined with remnants of other tribes or migrated to Cuba when Spain ceded Florida to England in 1763.

POST CALUSA ERA

Maps produced in the early 1800s do not specifically identify the island as Marco, but do indicate Marco or Malco — as it was often interchanged — for the river and passageway leading in from the Gulf of Mexico.

Records indicate that little development occurred on the island until the 1870s although a visitor, John Lee Williams, noted some growth and activity was taking place in Caxambas around 1824. Such efforts were likely carried out by the few remaining Spanish Indians — those of mixed Spanish and Indian descent — fishermen from neighboring islands and Cuba, explorers, hunters, refugees and runaway slaves.

The island and Southwest Florida, however, remained virtually uninhabited until after the Civil War when a handful of farmers and soldiers moved south to rebuild their lives on the raw, mosquito-infested Florida frontier.

The first arrivals were squatters who began making their way down the peninsula around the 1860s in mule wagons, ox carts or sailboats. The island was a mangrove swamp with virtually no population, inaccessible and not a road to be found, but it did not deter the hardy pioneers who were determined to make a go of their new life.

The year 1870 was around the corner and the dawn of a new era would begin — one that would produce dramatic change in both lifestyle and landscape. It would be spearheaded in the years to come by a handful of determined families whose island triumphs and tragedies would reverberate to this day.

Calusa paintings pages 27 & 28 produced by Ray Urbaniak.
Exploring Florida: A Social Studies Resource for Students and Teachers
Produced by Florida Center for Instructional Technology,
College of Education, University of South Florida © 2002.
Manataka American Indian Council — www.manataka.org

CALUSA MASKS COURTESY
PETER SOTTONG & TED MORRIS

OPPOSITE PAGE:
SPANISH/CALUSA MEETING
COURTESY BILL PERDICHIZZI
ARCHIVES

TOP: W.D. CAPT. BILL COLLIER, SEATED BACK ROW, CENTER, AND FAMILY MEMBERS ON THE STEPS OF THE MARCO HOTEL (TODAY'S OLDE MARCO INN)
LEFT TO RIGHT: AREA WHERE MARCO'S FOUNDER W.T. COLLIER LANDED (TODAY'S HIDEAWAY BEACH); ATLANTIC COAST LINE RAILWAY

COLLIER STEWARDSHIP

Long before glossy brochures depicted an ideal life here in paradise, a weary 55-year-old man, his wife and nine children steered a two-masted schooner onto a very different Marco Island.

When William Thomas (W.T.) Collier, Marco Island's founder, happened upon a sun-drenched, albeit mosquito-infested north shore in 1870 near present day Hideaway Beach, descendants say he was so taken by its sheer beauty that he declared it home.

As he anchored his beloved and battered *Robert E. Lee*, W.T., his wife Barbara and their young children could not have imagined the enormous challenges, triumphs and tragedies that would await them over the coming decades.

MARCO'S FOUNDER

W.T. was born in Tennessee in 1815. While his father had high hopes of a university education and a civil engineering career for his son, such aspirations were cut short by the economic realities of the day.

W.T. attended school through the age of 16 before landing work in a carriage manufacturing company. By the early 1840s, he became a millwright, finding work in North Carolina, Georgia and north Florida. If ever there was one to survive the ordeal of a pioneering way of life, it was W.T., because hardships for Marco's first settlers began virtually upon their arrival.

Within three months of landing on the island, a fire destroyed Collier's first home. He proceeded to build a palmetto shack. It too was destroyed, this time as a hurricane roared through the region. Determined to make it at the north end of the island, he settled on a home site in the very shell mound location that centuries before was the cultural mecca of the Calusa Indians (today's Olde Marco). He began farming in the muck-filled, wild land.

As the years passed, W.T. was finally able to purchase enough lumber to build what is believed to have been a boarding house, later run by one of his sons, W.D. Capt. Bill Collier, as the Marco Lodge. The home sat virtually where present-day Palm Street and Edington Place intersect at Olde Marco, although in 1964 it was moved from its location and transported to nearby Goodland.

W.D. CAPT. BILL COLLIER

W.T. and his wife would later add three more children to the fold before her tragic passing in 1900 at the age of 63. Barbara burned to death when she apparently spilled kerosene on hot coals she thought had been extinguished. The fire jumped rapidly to her clothing and engulfed her. Two years later, on Oct. 30, 1902, W.T. died of natural causes on his beloved island. He was 87.

While W.T. and Barbara ultimately raised 12 children — many of whom sought their fortunes elsewhere — none would thrive in the environment better than their second child, one of six boys, who was in his late teens when he landed on the island with his father by his side.

ENTREPRENEURIAL CAPTAIN BILL

Present day entrepreneurs would envy the foresight and business acumen attributed to Capt. Bill. He would successfully dabble in various interests, from boat building and farming to shipping and store ownership.

He opened a hotel, which still stands in Olde Marco today, and invented a prolific clam-dredging machine. His resume also included two terms

as a county commissioner and, after the tragic drowning of three of his boys, he put pen to paper in grief and authored a number of anti-religious pamphlets to cope with his pain.

Born in Quincy, Fla., on Sept. 20, 1852, Capt. Bill began his adult life at the north end of the island with a thirst for adventure and accomplishment. He opened a store on the Marco waterfront, and long before the modern day developers, Capt. Bill sized up the island's enormous tourism potential. It prompted him to construct the Marco Hotel despite the fact not a single road led to or off the island.

He married Margaret McIlvaine of Cedar Keys in 1880, a decade after landing on Marco. The couple had eight children before Margaret died in 1896, at the age of 38, while giving birth to a stillborn child. A year later, Captain Bill, in need of a wife to look after his young children, exchanged vows with Mary Shaw, who in turn needed a husband and a father for her daughter Camilla.

Capt. Bill also earnestly worked in the coastal sailing trade, operating a boat service that carried Collier produce, other fresh food and freight between Marco, Key West and Tampa. He would expand his business interests to include a shipyard that sold vessels to clients in Key West, Miami and Naples.

He grew squash, tomatoes and cabbages and even tried his hand growing pineapples and oranges. He also planted 5,000 coconut palms on the island. He became the second postmaster in the county in 1888. Marco at the time was part of Lee County, although, erroneously, postal officials named it "Malco" in the belief that there was another Marco in Florida. Capt. Bill's reward for bringing the postal service to the region? He had to pay for the service out of his own pocket for a year.

Press accounts of the era reveal that the island's first school was opened temporarily — thanks to Capt. Bill — in 1888. That same year, with Capt. Bill's assistance, the three-room Marco Village School opened permanently with a Miss Murdock teaching 15 pupils.

To archeologists and scholars in the late 1890s, he was known the world over for pulling from the Marco muck some of the most valuable Calusa Indian artifacts ever found. It prompted a subsequent dig by famed archaeologist Frank Hamilton Cushing in 1896. Cushing uncovered prized artifacts on land he dubbed "Court of the Pile Dwellers," including a wooden figurine referred to today as the Key Marco Cat. It is housed at the Smithsonian Institution.

JOY & SORROW

His legacy, however, was the lasting transformation of his sprawling home site into today's Olde Marco Inn, located on Palm Street. It was officially opened in 1896 as the Marco Hotel. Upon completion, it was truly a magnificent structure featuring 20 sleeping rooms, a parlor, dining room and two-story outhouse immortalized in a Ripley's *"Believe it or Not"* newspaper column as the only one of its kind in the world. Even the chairs took on a look of luxury — they were upholstered. Because of subsequent additions and renovations, including cottages on the property, Capt. Bill eventually was forced to hike the room rate from $1 to a whopping $2 per night. One of his first guests was Cushing, according to descendants.

Capt. Bill also had a hand in creating Marco's first tourist park. It was located on the waterfront, behind his store, and during the Great Depression it was occupied by "tin canners" (seasonal tourists). As the general store hangers-on would say: "They came in the winter with a $2 dollar bill and a blue shirt and wouldn't change either until they went back home in the spring."

Capt. Bill's life was not without torment.

In April 1877, his 23-year-old brother Benjamin fell overboard in a storm on a boat helmed by Capt. Bill and drowned. Benjamin was but three weeks away from his wedding day. It fell on Capt. Bill to break the news to Benjamin's bride. His mother burned to death on the island and later one of his five girls, Agnes, died in an island fire at the age of 16.

TOP: LEFT TO RIGHT:
MARCO HOTEL, CIRCA 1920s
W.D. CAPT. BILL COLLIER
DOXSEE CLAM CANNERY

Nothing matched the horrible pain and agony, however, of losing his three sons on the same day in March, 1898. At the helm of his boat, *Speedwell*, and a storm brewing in the Florida Keys, Capt. Bill's vessel capsized just miles from its destination, drowning his three boys and six other passengers from Connecticut who were all locked in a cabin. It was one of the worst tragedies to befall anyone in the area. His sons - George (8 years old), Thomas (6) and Wilmer (4) – were the first local residents buried at the Marco Island Cemetery.

"My wife didn't want me to take the boys to Key West," recounted Capt. Bill to an author almost four decades after the incident. "But I thought the trip would get them used to the sea, so they could take my place when they were old enough … at the last minute, a Presbyterian missionary preacher asked to go along. He'd been sailing around the islands, holding services here and there and sort of freeloading on anybody who'd take him in. I said he could go, and it was the worst mistake I ever made."

Capt. Bill would later reveal that he requested the boys and the Connecticut family to retire to the safe confines of the cabin. With the storm howling, the rain and seas heavy, he then handed the preacher an ax and ordered him to cut the main sail. The preacher did not do as he was instructed, however. Instead, he dropped to his knees and prayed moments before the boat capsized. The two deckhands, the preacher, and Capt. Bill survived the ordeal although it took a full day before they were rescued by a steamer.

THE DOXSEE CONNECTION

Though the tragedy inflicted a deep wound, Capt. Bill nonetheless soldiered on. In 1908, he invented a motorized clam-dredging machine to assist the island's fledgling industry. The Elmer S. Burnham Cannery to the south in Caxambas had already opened its doors in 1904.

Seeing the enormous potential his dredge could bring the region in employment and profits, he urged clam industry giant J. Harvey Doxsee of New York to visit Marco. With a little arm-twisting, Doxsee was sold.

In 1911, on land owned by Capt. Bill, Doxsee opened the island's second cannery operation.

Virtually overnight, the island had two significant industries that provided steady employment for men, women *and* children. Clam beds — like fish teeming in the emerald blue waters of the Gulf and waterways — were believed to be bottomless pits. The success of the two operations prompted the Atlantic Coast Line Railway to begin service on June 27, 1927. Trains would eventually make two trips to the island daily to pick up the clams.

J. HARVEY DOXSEE

Capt. Bill would build a second dredge but the demand for clam products was still so great that the two cannery operations couldn't keep pace.

Doxsee's popularity also grew with the community. He became the first chairman of the Board of Public Instruction and a Collier County commissioner. The cannery that bore his name became one of the island's first polling stations. The one ferry that linked the island to the mainland in 1912 was named after him. It was capable of transporting one vehicle at a time, arriving in Marco village, until a new four-car ferry was operational. When state legislators incorporated the island Collier City in 1927 to make way for ambitious development plans primarily to the south in Caxambas, Doxsee became its first and only mayor. While the intent was to name the entire island Collier City — after W.T. Collier — residents still referred to their communities as Marco village and Caxambas although to outsiders the two communities were briefly known as Collier City North (Marco village) and Collier City South (Caxambas).

COLLIER CITY SIGN

BIG PLANS DOOMED

Renaming the island was the brainchild of the San Marco Corporation, a New York-based syndicate that planned to develop Marco village in the late 1920s after acquiring the land from Capt. Bill. The corporation divided the village into 525 lots with an asking price of $6,000 to $10,000 each. The selling of the island to the world's rich and elite began, and a huge regatta was staged in 1927 to encourage sales. Company directors built the *Lulu Belle*, a 28-foot boat designed for deep sea fishing and sightseeing excursions. Brochures were published extolling the virtues of building a home "in one of the most beautiful parts of Florida" and the hotel, that would become the development's focal point, was portrayed in poetic terms:

> *"Operation of the Marco Hotel and Cottage Colony has been with but one idea in view, namely, on a basis where guests will meet substantial people of refinement, and to provide comfort and simple, courteous service with good wholesome food ... we have established ourselves with as fine a clientele that any resort can boast, a clientele that appreciates*

> *the elite, yet who come here to throw off the yoke of business and social cares, here there is no pretense, no fan fare, just a small group of fine people enjoying the lure of the islands and unexplored waterways, teeming with fish and the beautiful shell-lined shallow beaches, under the glow of a tropical sun."*

Despite the glowing publicity, the project was doomed by the looming Great Depression. The subsequent years weren't any better for residents either.

Clam beds were drying up. Capt. Bill's two clam dredges were prolific, gathering 300 to 500 bushels per day, but that would also prove to be one of the factors in the industry downfall. The Burnham factory closed its doors in 1929 — the same year their clam dredge sank — but Doxsee came to the rescue, agreeing to take over the Burnham operation in an effort to keep local residents employed during the Great Depression. In 1932, however, a hurricane destroyed the Burnham site.

Other bad news would follow. The railway pulled out in 1942. There simply weren't enough clams to make it worthwhile. Although some trips were still made to pick up clams over the next two years, the final train chugged across the Marco River trestle bridge for the last time in 1944.

Doxsee's plant suffered a similar fate. He hung on until 1947 before he too closed his doors. Finding less than 200 bushels of clams a day, Doxsee pulled the plug on his operation and sold the facility for salvage. He was 85 when he passed away in 1963.

What of Capt. Bill? After selling his Marco village holdings, he retired to Fort Myers, although he would continue to provide food and supplies to settlers in the area by sailing his ships between Key West and Tampa. He died in 1934, just hours after arguing about religion and actually exchanging fisticuffs with two young evangelists on a Fort Myers street, still heartbroken over the death of his three sons decades earlier. He was 82.

BURNHAM CLAM FACTORY

THE BARFIELDS

JAMES BARFIELD

James Madison Barfield and his wife Tommie Camilla Stephens Barfield packed a one-two punch and will likely go down in the annals of island history as the most influential power couple, then or now.

They began their tireless community efforts virtually upon their respective arrivals near the turn of the 20th century and would go on to shape their Caxambas community to the south the way the Collier family orchestrated life in Marco village to the north.

JAMES BARFIELD: TOMMIE MEETS HER MATCH

History may tell us that behind every great man is a great woman. In Tommie Barfield's case, she was a great woman blessed with a loving, highly supportive great man behind her.

James and his brother, Benjamin, made their way to Caxambas in 1892 via Georgia and Alabama intrigued by the south end of the island and its raw, untapped potential. Although they were greeted by mosquitoes and sand flies, they were determined to make a life on the land. That they did, operating a sizable farming operation, including pineapples for the Key West and northern markets.

Unlike Marco village, which was founded in 1870 by 55-year-old W.T. Collier, records do not reveal who founded the Caxambas community. Tony Roberts and Charles Johnson were believed to be the first settlers, but each had moved on when the Barfield brothers arrived.

By 1901, when A.T. Stephens and his family arrived in Caxambas with their 13-year-old daughter, Tommie, James Barfield was enjoying the spoils of his farming labor.

Born Jan. 29, 1867, in Sunnyside, Ga., James was as adept an entrepreneur in Caxambas as W. D. Capt. Bill Collier was at the north end of the island. James played a pivotal role in bringing industry to the south end of the island. He induced the Elmer S. Burnham clam cannery to operate out of Caxambas in 1904 and, later that same year, he opened a general store on the Caxambas waterfront. It catered daily to the local residents

and fishermen. He also opened the Caxambas post office in 1904 and became its first postmaster. As fate would have it, he hired A. T. Stephens — his future father-in-law — to be the first mail carrier.

He would remain a bachelor until the age of 39 when, on July 31, 1906, he took the hand of a bride 21 years his junior. The age gap hardly made a difference as Barfield, and his 18-year-old wife, Tommie, would begin a union punctuated by a strong desire to improve their lot in life and the lives of others.

HEIGHTS HOTEL

They lived high atop Caxambas on present-day Indian Hill in a grand structure that opened its doors in 1908 and became known as the Heights Hotel. Later, the couple acquired other properties, including the Marco Lodge at the north end of the island, and forged both a personal and working relationship with their one true island peer: Capt. Bill.

TOMMIE'S SPIRIT TAKES FLIGHT

Tommie, however, had no equal. Highly respected by friend and foe alike, she was one of the most prominent individuals of her era in Southwest Florida. She constantly sought a better life for her family - consisting of daughters Elsie, Elva and Ava - and all those who called the island and her beloved Caxambas home.

"Tommie Barfield was a woman of great integrity," said Elizabeth "Betsy" Perdichizzi, co-author of *A Girl Called Tommie, Queen of Marco*

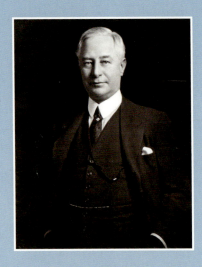

Barron Gift Collier was a New York City and Southwest Florida icon before his death in 1939 at the age of 65. He purchased close to one million acres of local real estate between 1921 and 1922 including 90 per cent of Marco Island. At the time of his passing, he was the largest land owner in the state. He was the driving force behind the completion of the Tamiami Trail from Tampa to Miami in exchange for state legislators naming his huge land purchases, Collier County, in 1923. A high school dropout who acquired a fortune in streetcar advertising in New York, Collier served from 1922 to 1925 as a special deputy police commissioner in charge of the Public Safety Bureau in New York City. The white or yellow line in the center of streets/highways for the guidance of traffic was his idea and he was the catalyst behind America joining the International World Police, more commonly known today as Interpol. Collier sought to build a major sea port and horse racing track here at the south end of the island but the Great Depression scuttled his ambitious plans. After the tragic passing of two of his adult-aged sons, his lone heir, Barron Jr., tried to sell the island to the State of Florida as a nature preserve in the early 1960s but the state turned him down — the $1 million price tag was simply too steep. Barron Jr. and his advisors would ultimately hammer out a $7 million deal in the mid-1960s with the Mackle brothers, Miami-based developers Elliott, Robert and Frank Jr., who would go on to develop Marco Island's modern era.

Island. "This was a woman with only a third grade education who went on to become, in essence, an extremely successful female lobbyist in an age when women didn't even have the right to vote."

She was a tireless worker, often driving her car through the wee morning hours to and from Fort Myers to lobby Lee County Commissioners (Collier County, in which Marco sits, was not named until 1923) for better roads, schools and other amenities sorely lacking on the island. Commissioners often placed her last on the agenda, making Tommie sit through day-long meetings before her issues were even discussed.

Her perseverance would pay off. Commissioners eventually approved the construction of a road from Naples to Marco (completed in 1912), a ferry to cross the Marco River, landing in Marco village (also in 1912), and, if she commenced building a road from Marco village to Caxambas, the commission would likely assist at a later date.

With shovels in tow, Tommie and a handful of helpers began the island's first road connecting its two communities. She would later lobby for a four-car ferry and, it too, was approved.

BARRON'S BIG PLANS

Her greatest triumph, however, occurred when she joined forces with Barron Gift Collier to create Collier County in 1923. The millionaire streetcar advertising magnate from New York saw great potential in Southwest Florida and promptly purchased over one million acres of local real estate between 1921 and 1922, including 90 percent of Marco Island. Just before his land-buying spree, Barron had met with the Barfields to purchase the Heights Hotel in 1920.

The Barfields themselves saw potential in land development in 1921. They actually platted and subdivided their Caxambas holdings and created the J. M. Barfield Subdivision. Waterfront lots were offered for just $200 but there were no takers.

Still, Barron was quite impressed by what he had seen in the couple, especially Tommie's tenacious resolve. When he proceeded to lobby state legislators to create a new county south of Fort Myers in his name — based on the argument that Lee County was not meeting the needs of all Southwest Florida residents — Tommie was hand-picked to lead the cause.

According to a media report, Tommie eloquently dazzled legislators about Barron's "big plans" for the area. It worked but with one caveat: Collier received his county as long as he would finance and build the Tamiami Trail from Tampa to Miami.

"She told of the plans of Barron G. Collier, great advertising tycoon, but every member of that committee realized the selling job that had been done by Mrs. Barfield," proclaimed a Fort Myers newspaper at the time. "The bill to create Collier County was bitterly fought by Lee County, from which it was carved, but the lady who was affectionately known as the 'Queen of Marco Island' convinced the legislators to override all objections."

On May 8, 1923, Florida Governor Cary A. Hardee signed legislation creating Collier County. And, what exactly were Barron's "big plans" talked about so fondly by Tommie?

Not since the island's founding in 1870 had anyone remotely attempted to make way for progressive, island-wide development. Barron would be that man.

He envisioned a major sea port that would have been located in today's Barfield Bay area. A three-mile channel would have been dredged through Caxambas Pass to allow American and foreign vessels to oper-ate. The port would have linked Marco Island to such harbors as Havana,

TOP: BARRON COLLIER, THIRD FROM LEFT, LOOKS ON AS GOVERNOR CARY A. HARDEE CREATES COLLIER COUNTY WITH THE STROKE OF A PEN IN 1923

RIGHT: MAP OF COLLIER CITY. NOTE THE OVAL WHERE A HORSE RACING TRACK WAS PLANNED AT THE SOUTHWESTERN END OF THE ISLAND AND THE ANTICIPATED DEEP WATER PORT IN TODAY'S BARFIELD BAY

PRELIMINARY PLAN
COLLIER CITY
FLORIDA
SCALE 1" = 3000 FT.

Cuba and Key West. The island itself would be named Collier City, not for Barron — he had a county named for him, after all — but for W.T. Collier, the island's founder.

A lumber mill was slated to produce about 300,000 board feet daily which in turn would support a host of other island businesses. Some 3,000 residents were expected to make their home on the island with, as Barron imagined, the population growing until Collier City ranked as the top metropolitan area on Florida's west coast.

A surveyor who worked for Barron's interests estimated that Collier City would grow as quickly as Miami. According to a newspaper account, the surveyor said: "If favored with one of keen vision backed with sufficient finances, there seems no reason to doubt that Collier City is destined to outstrip in population, in wealth, in growth and in power every town or city now on the west coast of Florida."

The looming Great Depression put an end to Collier City before it began. Barron would live until 1939 when he passed away just 10 days before his 66th birthday.

EDUCATION IS KEY

Tommie's greatest influence may very well have been in the lives of children throughout the island and fledgling Collier County. Education was of paramount importance to her and she lobbied heavily for schools, educational materials and even teachers.

Caxambas was the site of two and perhaps even three schools over the years, although many times classes were actually held in the kitchen of Tommie's home. Some published accounts refer to a Caxambas school house in need of repairs as early as 1892. Another account states a school was built in 1898. Although descendants can't pinpoint the exact date, by the 1920s a structure served both the schooling and recreational

needs of the community. The school house/community center would later show movies, making it the island's first movie theater.

It wasn't until the late 1920s when the student population in Caxambas and Marco village was large enough to warrant the construction of a new and improved school to serve both communities. Long time residents believe that a man by the name of Scripps, a manufacturer of marine and gas engines who visited Caxambas from the northeast during the winter months, donated the land to build the facility. The four-room, two-story structure was named in his honor. Tommie, meanwhile, insisted that teachers become boarders in her new Caxambas home.

Governor Hardee formally recognized Tommie's work in the education field in 1923 when he appointed her Collier County's first Superintendent of Public Instruction.

Tommie also found time to broaden her entrepreneurial interests beyond the region. She made candy and jellies — orange peel, orange marmalade and guava — which she sold across the United States and Europe. She named them Elsie Brand after one of her three daughters, and the boat that delivered the candy and jellies to market was named *Elva Lee* after another daughter. Amazingly, besides her numerous interests, she found time in the mid-1930s to operate one of Southwest Florida's largest apiaries with associate George Lowe. By the early 1940s, the apiary was producing 60,000 pounds of honey annually.

ABOVE: TOMMIE BARFIELD
LEFT: SCRIPPS SCHOOL, CAXAMBAS

James, meanwhile, served on the Board of County Commissioners for 20 years, even sitting in on the first Collier County board meeting in 1923. Twenty years later, "Uncle Jim," as he was affectionately known, passed away in his Caxambas home. He was 76. Collier County Commissioners passed a resolution in tribute to him on Dec. 6, 1943.

It stated:

"... the brightest days of his splendid life were dominated by his limit-less faith in his fellow man and in the future of Collier County and by his optimistic courage and determination to assist in and further the development of Collier County and the state of his adoption, which faith and determination neither reverses nor the weight of advancing years could daunt or prove effectual in blunting the edge of his splendid courage ... "

Tommie would pass away in 1950 at the age of 62. Her descendants believe she was suffering from Alzheimer's disease.

Collier County officials, as they had done for James years earlier, paid tribute to her extraordinary life.

"As the years pass and the historians delve into the history and progress of Collier County, they will find indelibly written on practically every page from the beginning of the county in 1923 to 4 p.m. Friday, Nov. 17, 1950, the name of a living, vibrating being who stood pre-eminent among the citizenry of the county for progress: fiscal, social and educational. As a member of the board of public instruction from the beginning of the county until her illness prior to her demise, Mrs. Tommie C. Barfield exemplified the highest ideals of good government, good citizenship and progressive thought. Steadfast in her demands on both county and state government, the dominant force of her personality was felt by the capital at Tallahassee and the board of county commissioners of Lee County before the formation of Collier County and as chairman of the board of public instruction of Collier County by the county officials, until her people and their needs were felt and recognized."

Tommie Barfield Elementary School opened in her honor six years later, in 1956.

TOP: BARFIELD HOME, 1922
BOTTOM: BARFIELD BOARDING HOUSE

Two of her daughters would carry on where their mother left off. Elsie married twice, taught school on the island and served as postmaster. Elva married Robert "Grits" Griffis, ran the G & G Mercantile Store on the Marco waterfront — which Capt. Bill formerly owned — built the Islander Motel at Marco, served as postmaster and was appointed to Collier County's Board of Public Instruction through 1963. Elsie and Elva have since passed away. Ava died in a Christmas Eve car accident in 1932. She was 22.

A MARCO LIFE RE-VISITED

It took a special breed of person to live on Marco Island's raw frontier. The pioneers, those who arrived and eked out a living here from 1870 until the modern era began in the mid 1960s, had few if any conveniences.

Newspaper accounts have painted a challenging existence for those who sought such a life but a recent discovery of a diary and other priceless handwritten letters offers a unique glimpse into a very different Marco Island than the one we enjoy today.

Doctors Louis and Mary Olds arrived here with their three young daughters, Orida, Saloma and Rosalie, in 1903. Highly educated, Mary had earned a Bachelor in Literature at Smith College in 1884 before attending Woman's Medical College of Pennsylvania, becoming one of the first women to receive a medical degree. The pair took post-graduate courses in homeopathic medicine. They were members of the New Church as were many of the intellectual elite in Philadelphia.

Upon their island arrival — it is not known why they left their refined, cultured lifestyle for the rugged challenges of Marco - they found themselves among unschooled and semi-literate fishermen, farmers, business people and charter boat captains. The Olds felt quite apart from their neighbors because of the differences in their background, culture and education yet living on the island forged a common bond between them.

DIARY REFLECTIONS

In fact, as discovered recently by island author Elizabeth "Betsy" Perdichizzi, Mary and her daughters kept diaries and wrote sensitive letters about their lives here.

"Dear '84," Mary explained to her 1884 graduating classmates in a letter dated 1905. "It is like stepping into the world our grandparents and great grandparents knew 100 – 200 years ago. I don't worry

about which new refrigerator to buy, but how to preserve food without ice or electricity in our long tropical summers!"

The Olds settled into a two-story frame house on the bank of the Marco River, possibly located where present-day retailer Kay's on the Beach sits on Bald Eagle Drive. After several years, wrote Mary in her diary, life here began to improve.

"Our house has been enlarged by the addition of a kitchen, so that I no longer have the rain trickling down the back of my neck while I prepare our dinner during the rainy season."

Pesky bugs, flies, insects and dreaded mosquitoes became unwanted visitors almost daily for the pioneers. Early settlers smeared lamp oil on their window screens to especially keep mosquitoes at bay. The screens, however, had to be cleaned often to allow a welcomed breeze to sweep through houses.

Mary briefly yet humorously mentioned mosquitoes in a letter dated 1905. "Just now we are having mortal conflict with mosquitoes — this is the height of their season . . . our insect pests are not injurious to the health, although, as Dr. Olds says, very hard on the temper."

SICKNESS & HEALTH

There were no amenities for sick pioneers on Marco Island, noted Mary, when writing about her own illness in March 1907.

"I was attacked by a serious illness, and for three months we certainly did have a hard time, all of us," she wrote. "Intestinal obstruction with symptoms resembling those of appendicitis was followed by peritonitis, and for a time my life hung in the balance. Those of you who have known terror of such troubles in your families, even with all the resources of civilization at your service, can perhaps imagine what we had to undergo here in the wilderness with no hospitals, no nurses, no servants, no proper nourishment, even, for a sick person."

OLDS HOMESTEAD

"When the worst danger was over we had to fight starvation, fresh milk seemed to be the only thing that I craved or could take, and this in a land in which cows are few and far between. Dr. Olds sent frantically in all directions for milk, but the cows had all gone dry, finally he got a tiny quantity each day by going ten miles in his launch after it — all the morning yield of a Florida cow."

The times were tougher still, for others.

Wiley and Vergie Dickerson would bury three of their seven children in the Marco Island Cemetery. Norma Janice, a baby, died after accidentally drinking fuel; five-year old Shera Lavinia succumbed to diphtheria; and, most heart-breaking, baby Donnell tumbled out of a car while her parents were rushing Shera to a hospital in Fort Myers for life-saving treatment. The handmade, concrete-heart headstone in the cemetery, crafted by father Wiley reads: "Here Lies our Heart."

A number of other babies suffering from a host of maladies would sadly endure the same fate, further testament to how tough it was to live and be cared for here.

SUSTENANCE OPTIONS

Food options were often tied to the seasons.

In February 1910, Mary wrote: "Our staple food for many weeks at this time of year are avocados (alligator pears), they really take the place of meat, and are wonderfully satisfying & delicious; & we have the finest I have ever tasted with fine mangoes, guavas, sea grapes, cocoa plums, bananas, myrtle berries etc. & products made from some of them — we have luxuries indeed . . . but how to keep things without ice in our long tropical summer (the secret is judicious re-cooking)."

Neighbors, the George Eubanks family, kept pigs about a mile up the road from the Olds family. Every so often, recounted Mary, the pigs would run wild through the swamps. When locals encountered a stray they would tell a member of the Eubanks family who would invariably come to catch the stray pig and bring it home.

Saloma, meanwhile, would go on to raise chickens in her backyard. "I have quite a little farm of my own now," she wrote. "I have twenty-nine Peking ducks and forty-two Rhode Island Red chickens. The ducks have the whole bay to roam in." Saloma also noted that one of her sisters, Rosalie, had seven chickens and was expecting to receive a pair of geese.

Added Mary in yet another letter to her friends: "Our chickens are developing into a business, and the world of eggs has provided food for themselves as well as for us. We had bloom on some orange and grapefruit trees (budded less than two years ago). We hope for some fruit for our own use at least this year. Our table improves as Dr. Olds learns better how to utilize the natural resources of the country in fish, oysters, game, etc. In the past two months he has been building himself a launch. Now that he is proudly navigating the waters in said launch, he assures me that we shall enjoy everything obtainable for miles around."

THE ALLURE OF MARCO ISLAND

A decade after the family's arrival, the allure of the island still beckoned and it was not lost on 15-year-old Saloma who, in July 1914, wrote, "I have just come in from seeing some beautiful sights, it has been raining hard and it is lightning everywhere; north; south and west and overhead. Not only flashes of light but rivers of fiery brightness . . . what fireworks! There was lightning at one of the four points of the compass every half minute — except the east, where the beautiful, peaceful, full moon shone out her radiance upon the earth . . . "

"Last night about nine o'clock (sister) Rosalie and I went out on the dock; and Oh! What a sight met our eyes! The water was literally a garden of stars; there was not a breath of air or a cloud in the sky; every large star in the heavens was reflected perfectly in the water; we could even see them twinkle in the water. The whole great dipper was in the water and the big Venus and Jupiter in the east. Even the Milky Way all across the sky could be seen in the water. And not only the stars but also Beethoven! It seemed like a fairyland. Mama played the second and third movements of Opus 14 Number 1 . . . That sonata is a wonderfully beautiful and poetic one, full of deep feeling and yet in a way, dreamy. Ok, poetic is the word! Oh, that Beethoven and those stars made a paradise of beauty!"

MOONLIGHT OVER MARCO

MARY OLDS IN HER GARDEN

SURVIVAL MODE

Such moments may very well have been the impetus for many to forge ahead.

Louis would go on to plant mangoes, lemon and avocado trees, as well as celery, onions, peppers, cauliflower and strawberries to supplement his medical practice.

"Dr. Olds has bought some new land recently," wrote Mary. "We were all pressed into service for half of each week to help pack the tomatoes for shipment. In addition to the usual housework it was really too much; and when Jack Frost made one of his rare visits here, and nipped the tomatoes I believe we were all more glad than sorry, in spite of the business loss. This new land, by the way, includes one of the famous shell mounds attributed to the prehistoric Indians, and on this very shell mound these tomatoes were raised "shell-land" being in great demand for such purposes."

Local farmers produced enormous vegetables in the mild sub-tropical climate and rich shell-mound soil. The Collier family, living at the north end of the island where Calusa Indians had lived centuries before, built up to 70 crates a day to ship their produce, according to historian Charlton Tebeau in *Florida's Last Frontier*.

"Watermelons weighing forty pounds apiece, and single heads of cabbage, weighing as much as eighteen and one-half pounds," wrote Tebeau. "They continued to ship what vegetables they didn't keep for themselves south to Key West and north along the west coast to Tampa and Cedar Key. The Colliers were the first people in Southwestern Florida to ship vegetables north for the winter market."

Pineapple fields were flourishing here as well. John Foley Horr operated a pineapple industry just southeast of Marco on a nearby island (today's high-end development known as Key Marco). Also south, in Caxambas, brothers Benjamin and James Barfield raised pineapples and had a packing house. Frederick Ludlow, however, laid claim to the largest pinery, one year raising a million pineapples over 200 acres.

WELCOMED VISITORS

The Olds family found companionship with Mr. & Mrs. Walter N. Halderman of Palm Cottage, their two sons W. B. and Bruce Halderman, and guests at the hotels in Naples and Marco. Long before the island became almost a daily magnet for the jet set, Mary hosted beach picnics

for wealthy and prominent families visiting the region, among them: Gifford Pinchot, Governor of Pennsylvania; William Temple Hornaday of the Bronx Zoo; A. W. Dimock, author of children's books and his son Julian Dimock, a photographer, among others. The family entertained their guests after dinner, often with music and dancing, as Mary held court at the piano.

Islanders, too, celebrated with a variety of entertainment. They held a May Day celebration in 1927 to celebrate the island's new name. Collier City had just been incorporated by the state legislature. The whole island, it seems, turned out. A band played on the newly constructed bandstand on the Marco Hotel grounds. Swimming, fishing, and diving contests were held in the river. Mattie, niece of island icon Tommie Barfield, was selected May Queen. Children were outfitted in their best clothes. The celebration lasted almost as long as Collier City. Ambitious development plans for the island, headed by streetcar advertising tycoon Barron Gift Collier, failed to materialize. Add the looming Great Depression and Collier City was scuttled.

Mary preferred to home school her daughters rather than send them to Miss Lettie Nut's class in Marco village. Mary taught the girls Latin,

TOP: LEFT TO RIGHT: LUDLOW PINEAPPLE FIELD; ORIDA OLDS

Greek, German, Hebrew, literature and music. She wrote: "People have come from miles around, who had never seen or heard a piano, to ask me to play. The neighbors are inclined to classify me as lazy, because I sit on the porch so much, teaching the girls."

In 1928, to the south in Caxambas, the Scripps School opened. A total of 73 students from Marco village and Caxambas attended classes that year.

FOND FAREWELLS

Around this time the Olds family would ultimately make their way back to Pennsylvania — it is not known why they departed Marco Island — but after two-plus decades in the rugged wilderness one could easily make a case for such a move. Each family member has since passed on but the diaries and letters recently discovered shed an important light on Marco that has not been shed before.

By the late 1940s, having lived in the Barfield boarding house while teaching school here for about a decade, local resident Thelma Heath was also leaving the island but not before she too put pen to paper in reflection. Her sentiments could easily have been attributed to members of the Olds family. Thelma wrote a poignant farewell in her 1949 memoir:

"On the island, we had been living in an age rooted in the last century; isolated from medical help and shopping; in a boarding house with no privacy or locked doors; with mosquitoes, sand flies, no electricity, kerosene lamps, gasoline irons, kerosene stove and refrigerator, poor drinking water; and rub-a-dub washboard laundry at times. Our new home in Naples, only eighteen miles away was a giant step into the Twentieth Century."

The modernization the Olds family and Thelma had each sought, however, was around the corner and — for better or worse — the island and its residents would soon be transformed forever.

SALOMA OLDS

Will Be Missed, But—

ld-Timers At Marco Welcome Progre

Plans for Marco Island Submitted by Developer

Mackles Announce Plans in Detail

Stunning Plan For Development Of Marco Island

10 Models of the $15,000 to $25,000 Marco Island Homes

Bridge Will Link This Road Stub to Main

News

Model Homes

adied on Marco

lorida As Ideal Place To Invest

pace-Age Li

e Total Now
ast-Growing

Marco Readies for City of 50,000

Resort future for Marco Island

Mixed Emotions Greet Plan For Marco Island

1st Model Ho
Readied on M

he 3 Mackle Brothers Re
istory Of Real Estate In

Profile

THE MACKLE BROTHERS

Three brothers, not easily charmed, fell in love with Florida's ultimate piece of swamp land the minute they saw it.

The Deltona Corporation executives had just walked onto the north end of Marco Island's majestic white sand beach for the very first time — it was 1962 — but none could utter a single word.

As a hot sun beat down on them Elliott, the oldest, removed his suit coat; Robert tugged on his tie; Frank Jr. wiped beads of sweat from his brow.

The famous Miami-based developers — the mighty Mackle brothers — were in awe of the sheer undeveloped landscape before their eyes.

Frank Jr., the youngest and most gregarious of the group, was the first to break the silence.

"I can't believe what I'm seeing," he said, turning to his brothers with a broad grin across his face. Elliott, Robert and two other executives, Neil Bahr and Jim Vensel, nodded their heads in agreement.

MARCO ISLAND'S SPELL

The Mackle brothers, Bahr and Vensel — each has since passed on — weren't the first to be wowed by Marco Island's charm and they certainly won't be the last.

Centuries before, Marco was the domain of fierce Calusa Indian warriors. Spanish explorers would soon follow and, later in the annals of island history, Marco would unabashedly cast her spell on a host of families who fled the Civil War seeking new frontiers.

While battles with neighboring tribes and the Spanish conquerors decimated their numbers, it was actually disease spread by the weary cross Atlantic travelers which wiped the Calusa entirely from Marco. Whoever followed in their footsteps to build on their sacred ground, according to local legend, would be cursed.

This far-fetched scenario was the furthest thing from the minds of the five savvy businessmen some 50-plus years ago. It was now their turn to be mesmerized by the beauty and potential before them.

"We were stunned standing on that beach," recalled Bahr. "Absolutely stunned. It was so magnificent. It was almost too good to be true."

The wide-eyed group saw hotels and condominiums emerging from the mangroves. Inland, they pictured an intricate system of waterfront canals where none existed. In essence these men, not prone to folly, envisioned a development community like no other in U.S. history yet the task before them, rising out of the proverbial Florida swamp land, was daunting.

Just 150 residents called it home. Roads would have to be constructed, a water source found, sewers had to be installed, mosquitoes had to be controlled and an airport needed to be built for the visitors and potential home buyers who would share in their dream. And, while the Gulf of Mexico sparkled and the empty three-and-a-half mile crescent-shaped beach beckoned, Marco Island's location was remote.

Who would ever come?

"We had that beach, however, that amazing white-sand beach," said Bahr, the highly-respected sales executive affectionately dubbed "the fourth Mackle brother". "We knew it would be the focal point of all of our sales efforts . . . we just needed people to see it."

ALL IN THE FAMILY

The Mackle brothers knew a thing or two about Florida construction and development having learned the trade from their father. Frank Mackle Sr. was born in England in 1881 and soon ventured across the pond to New Jersey. By 1908, the same year Elliott was born, the elder Mackle opened a fledgling construction company in Jacksonville. Five years later, it was on to Atlanta where Robert and Frank Jr. were born.

LEFT: THE MACKLE BROTHERS WITH TRUSTED EXECUTIVE NEIL BAHR, AFFECTIONATELY DUBBED "THE FOURTH MACKLE BROTHER." FROM LEFT. BAHR, FRANK JR., ROBERT AND ELLIOTT

ABOVE; MACKLE BROTHERS CIRCA 1918, FROM LEFT, ELLIOTT, FRANK JR. AND ROBERT

FRANK MACKLE SR.

THE MACKLE BROTHERS, FROM LEFT, FRANK JR., ROBERT AND ELLIOTT

"Be the first on the job in the morning and the last to leave at night . . . build good houses . . . and don't build any monuments to yourselves," he said.

According to Elliot, the biggest virtue passed on by his father was telling the boys that they should not expect credit for being honest.

"Dad said you are *supposed* to be honest," he recalled.

Frank Sr. died in 1941 but his sons heeded his sage advice for the rest of their professional lives. Elliott would now take the helm of the family operations while Robert and Frank Jr. served as navy engineers.

Frank Sr. proceeded to build offices, apartments and hotels throughout Florida, Alabama, Georgia and Tennessee.

The brothers would learn their trade honestly enough from the ground up, mixing cement on jobsites during school vacations. Elliott and Robert would go on to study engineering and architecture at Washington and Lee University while Frank Jr. earned an engineering degree at Vanderbilt.

Frank Sr. and his talented sons would then set their sights on the South Florida market, building 20 low-cost homes in Delray Beach. The properties sold so quickly, Frank Sr. promptly abandoned commercial construction altogether and moved the family to West Palm Beach where, together, they would begin the next phase of their lives.

The elder Mackle did not mince words when it came to advising his sons about the family business.

During World War II they built the $18-million naval base at Key West, the naval air station in Brunswick, Georgia, and naval housing at Opa-Locka, west of Miami.

While they may not have been the first to recognize the growing importance of the housing market for the nation's retirees, they were the first to approach the subject with a degree of scientific curiosity.

Their interest in the senior citizen population was whetted in the late 1940s. As they built properties to cater to the pent up demand for GI homes they noticed that a surprising number of buyers turned out to be, not veterans, but elderly northerners who were approaching retirement age with a desire to flee the northern winters.

At the same time an economist colleague had been fascinated by this relatively new economic phenomenon: The growing numbers of senior citizens, solidly buttressed by Social Security annuities and pension funds. Here, the colleague argued, was a tremendous, potential housing market. It was pointed out that an estimated three million retired workers were even then drawing nearly $2 billion in Social Security

and other benefits. This total was expected to rise steadily until, by 1960, an estimated 12 million Americans were expected to be drawing regular monthly checks aggregating $10 billion.

Intrigued, the Mackles took out an ad in a popular national magazine, asking pointed questions: Are you planning to move when you retire? . . . Where would you move to? . . . Would you buy a retirement home? . . . What would you pay for it?

A MODERN DAY GOLD MINE

The data proved to be a modern day gold mine. They learned that seven out of 10 who replied to the ad would prefer to retire to Florida. They learned also that the average couple on Social Security could expect to retire with a regular monthly income of $160.

RIGHT: ELLIOTT, ROBERT
AND FRANK MACKLE JR.

TOP: JIM VENSEL

The brothers then turned to the Federal Housing Administration and asked what kind of a mortgage loan could a couple comfortably carry? And, they asked Vensel, their chief architect at the time, to design homes that could specifically be sold to couples living on Social Security payments. Vensel came up with a one bedroom model built to sell for $4,750 with payments running to about $300 annually. Larger models ran as high as $8,500.

"We made it possible for couples to buy a home for less each year than it would cost them to rent for a three-or four-week Florida winter vacation," said Elliott.

Elliott was noted for being able to find land to develop when a new project was planned. Robert was the financial genius who was also the point man when dealing with unions. Frank Jr. was gifted at public relations and had a knack for getting along with people from all walks of life. The elder brothers picked Frank Jr. to later become Deltona's president.

In practice, however, the company functioned as if it had three presidents. They shared the same large office and the services of a single secretary. Three huge, identical desks were positioned in a semi-circle. Regardless of which brother was in the office at any given time, he would speak on behalf of management. There would be no delays when a top level opinion was sought but each brother agreed that major, strategic decisions between them would have to be unanimous.

The business model worked to perfection.

"I may have had to have bumped a couple of heads together," Robert, the largest brother, joked with a reporter from the *St. Petersburg Times*. "But all decisions are unanimous."

"It's amazing, though, how much of our thinking coincided," added Frank Jr.

After the war, the brothers built attractive low-cost homes in Miami, West Palm Beach, Coral Gables and Bradenton and found themselves

51

squarely in the midst of the historic post-war housing shortage. Here was a crisis that called for boldness and imagination, virtues the Mackles had in abundance.

MARCO ISLAND'S BLUEPRINT

They launched Westwood Lakes, a suburb-sized community of 3,500 homes, built around man-made lakes west of Miami. Tamiami Gardens, Linden Gardens, Oakland Park, Grapeland Heights and Pompano Beach Highlands would soon follow.

They even took over an old coconut plantation on Key Biscayne, just south of Miami, and created a tropic island paradise of 1,000 medium cost homes — affectionately dubbed "Mackles" by their owners — complete with a picturesque shopping center and a plush resort hotel which would later become a hideaway for celebrities and the elite. The Key Biscayne effort would virtually become the blueprint for Marco Island.

National advertising, mail order home site sales on the Mackle's now incredulous "$10-down-and-$10-a-month" housing payment plan, a national network of franchised agents, sight-unseen home sales and many other Mackle innovations took the industry by storm.

Add more communities like Port Charlotte, Port St. Lucie and Sebastian Highlands, and the Mackles, according to *House & Home* magazine, became the nation's No. 1 homebuilder in 1958 and among the top four through 1961.

"Anyone searching for a secret formula in the success story of Miami's three Mackle brothers will seek in vain," gushed a Deltona press release. "They're no razzle-dazzle artists, this triumvirate . . . they earned their success in the toughest kind of competition . . . by working longer and harder than the next guy to give the customer more of what he was look-ing for: A better way of life in Florida at a price he could afford."

Just before walking Marco Island's beach for the first time in 1962, the brothers were in the midst of building their largest development,

some 15,000 acres of forested land in the lake and citrus country of east central Florida midway between Orlando and Daytona Beach. A contest was held to name the community. Deltona, which the brothers would later adopt as their company name, was born.

While receiving accolades for building quality developments, the Mackles were also becoming known for their kindness and generosity, agreeing to deals with customers based on trust, handshakes and honesty. No strings attached.

Encouraged by so many of these building successes in the state, the brothers would then turn their attention to Marco Island in the early 1960s.

The only way to get to the island without a boat at that time was by way of the old wooden swing bridge at Goodland. This had been re-assembled in 1938 from an even older bridge across the Caloosahatchee River at Fort Myers. Goodland itself was a scattering of small homes and trailers with a few businesses - what Floridians called a "fishing village" or "fish camp" in those days.

SHIFTING GEARS

Standing on Marco Island's beach in their suits and ties as they did in 1962, the Mackle brothers saw more, much more than just bricks-and-mortar in the sun. Frank Jr., especially, sensed that Marco Island's potential would be far greater than anything he and his brothers would ever develop. He knew the spectacular beach would indeed serve as a draw but it would not be the lone drawing card.

The sub-tropical climate would attract the masses, Frank Jr. reasoned, as would the promise of year-round golf, tennis, boating and fishing. He saw sprawling resort hotels, huge swimming pools and children building the perfect sand castles on an endless white-carpeted beach that featured the most beautiful shells he had ever seen.

A PORTRAIT OF FRANK MACKLE SR. HANGS BEHIND HIS SONS. ROBERT, FRANK JR. AND ELLIOTT, FROM LEFT, PLANNED A RESORT/LEISURE COMMUNITY FOR MARCO ISLAND UNLIKE ANY OTHER DEVELOPMENT IN U.S. HISTORY. THE BOLD NEW APPROACH IS OUTLINED BELOW:

"Rather than being aimed primarily at retirees, (Marco Island) is designed for a complete range of resort and leisure living – hotels, motels, apartments and extensive areas for homes. The company expects that as the community grows, its business and commercial life will expand too, and younger working families will comprise a sizable part of the population. However, it is expected that most of Marco Island's growth will derive from tourist activities and from the demand for second homes for vacation, weekend and other leisure use."

— Deltona Corporation Annual Report, 1964

Yet, not even these great visionaries could remotely fathom just how amazing Marco Island's geographic location would ultimately become for future residents and visitors to enjoy. The uninhabited Ten Thousand Island chain would stretch from Marco all the way down to the Florida Keys and the nearby Everglades, its sensitive ecosystem as magical as the island the Mackle brothers sought to develop, was literally in Marco's backyard

"I drove out to Marco and I couldn't believe what I saw," recounted Frank Jr., years later.

"I drove down State Road 92 and suddenly I saw this big half-moon beach with nothing there."

"The mosquitoes were horrendous and sent me running back to the car. There was no drinking water. The few people who lived there gathered rain water off the roof into a cistern. I thought it was amazing that no one had developed it."

Their newly branded company, the Deltona Corporation, would purchase virtually all of Marco Island for $7 million and, later, their reach extended to additional acres on adjoining islands and the mainland. As they had done in building so many other Florida projects, a strong, honorable work ethic and an abundance of soaring imagination would propel the dream.

"Truth be told: There was also a bit of apprehension among us before Marco Island was introduced," recalled Bahr. "Up to that time the Mackles had built retirement communities . . . here we would be shifting gears. Marco Island would be totally different from anything we had ever approached before."

Deltona's 1964 annual report featured a passage which outlined the bold new scenario for Marco:

$500 Million Development Planned for Marco Island

"Rather than being aimed primarily at retirees, (Marco Island) is designed for a complete range of resort and leisure living — hotels, motels, apartments and extensive areas for homes. The company expects that as the community grows, its business and commercial life will expand too, and younger working families will comprise a sizable part of the population. However, it is expected that most of Marco Island's growth will derive from tourist activities and from the demand for second homes for vacation, weekend and other leisure use."

Eager to share their spectacular find with the world, Elliott, 56 years old at the time, Robert, 52, and Frank Jr., 48, quickly secured the necessary building permits — it could not have been easier — and began re-shaping the Marco Island swamp.

Opening Day was around the corner. The sky's the limit. What could possibly go wrong?

CHICAGO TRIBUNE INSERT, JAN. 31, 1965

WHEN MODERN MARCO ISLAND OPENED ITS DOORS TO THE WORLD ON JAN. 31, 1965 OFFICIALS MANNING THE DELTONA SALES OFFICE WERE SWAMPED.
IT WAS A SIGN OF GOOD THINGS TO COME. THIS IS A RARE OPENING DAY PHOTOGRAPH. TODAY, THE SITE IS HOME TO MARCO'S CITY HALL COMPLEX.

PARADISE IS NOW OPEN

Modern Marco Island opened its doors on Jan. 31, 1965, under the crush of 25,000 visitors eager to secure their own piece of paradise.

Construction equipment was everywhere, dirt was blowing, and the scene appeared to be that of a barren island as opposed to the barrier paradise depicted in the shiny new promotional brochures.

Still, Deltona Corporation executives Elliott, Robert and Frank Mackle Jr., encouraged the future home owners and media representatives gathered that day to look beyond the obvious and to share in their dream.

"This is the most comprehensive and complex city building job undertaken by a single company," Frank Jr. told the visitors. "Before we are through at Marco Island – 10 to 20 years from now – this new Florida community will have 35,000 persons. We will spend well over half a billion dollars to develop this island and we believe this program to be the most significant in Florida since Carl Fisher built Miami Beach. It opens a wilderness to modern growth."

The Mackle brothers had no idea how many people would be interested in their little gem despite a $600,000 advertising blitz that included color newspaper supplements and full-page newspaper and magazine ads placed throughout the country. Bus placards, billboards and 700 radio and television spots lured prospective buyers to the island, as did advertising in Western Europe, Latin America and the Far East.

Mackle staff manning the new $85,000 administration/sales office could barely accommodate the hordes but it proved to be a sign of good things to come. Over the next 30 days, 50,000 inquiries would flood the office on San Marco Road, where the island's city hall complex stands today.

FESTIVE MOOD

The Opening Day mood was festive, to say the least. The Mackles were beaming having enjoyed a week of pre-launch parties on the island and in Naples with a cast of who's who in America.

Miami Herald social columnist Doris Reynolds joined dozens of fellow journalists covering the Marco Island opening. The scene, as penned by Reynolds, speaks for itself:

"… there was a large cocktail party at the Marco Beach Hotel, followed by an elaborate champagne dinner. Drinks and canapes were served around the pool, where the strains of an orchestra drifted across the beach. It was really a historic moment – the first time such goings on had happened on Marco Beach since the Calusa Indians had their feasts here. Mr. and Mrs. M. R. Mathews greeted guests in the stunning new lobby of Marco's first beach front facility. Billy Vessels and his very attractive wife were recognized by football fans. Billy, a member of the Deltona executive staff, is a former All-American from the University of Oklahoma. There were many distinguished members of the press there, including John Goldsmith, managing editor of House & Home magazine; James DeLong, architecture editor of House Beautiful, was there, as were the Morton Kails of New York. He is editor of the New York Journal American …"

MARCO WAS OFF AND RUNNING
AND SO WAS THE MACKLE PR MACHINE

Frank Jr. could not have been more proud of the Marco Island vision he and his brothers were unwrapping: "We are building a waterfront community that will embody all the best features – and more – of such famous resort and residential cities as Fort Lauderdale, Miami Beach and Palm Beach."

SOUTH PACIFIC STYLE

The Mackles envisioned a Polynesian-design theme for the island and it would fall on company architects Jim Vensel and Herb Savage to deftly handle the task. Vensel, Deltona's chief architect, had already mapped out the hundreds of street names where people would eventually settle and live out a vibrant retirement — he did this incredulously over the 1964 Memorial Day weekend — while Savage had been dispatched with his wife Emily to the South Pacific before drawing a single Marco Island property.

"We searched far and wide and studied the best ideas we could find for waterfront and leisure living and then we incorporated those ideas with our own to produce villas specifically designed to take advantage of Marco Island's unique beauty," said Vensel in an interview with the *Naples Sun*, just days before the opening.

The first canals and homes had been built. Savage designed 12 on the waterfront at Chestnut Court and 10 inland on Tahiti Road just east of the sales center. Brochures listed the waterfront homes from $19,800 to $41,500, depending on the homeowner request for one-to three-bedrooms and baths. The Tahiti Road models ranged in price from $14,900 to $23,500.

"The new models incorporate all of the knowledge and experience which the Mackle family has accumulated in over 56 years of building," said Frank Jr. "We have never built a finer selection of homes. From the beginning we have felt that only the best is good enough for Marco Island."

Opening Day home sites were listed in the $2,500 range for inside lots and from $5,495 to $16,000 for waterfront sites. The Mackle brothers had even completed a utility system featuring water treatment and a sewage disposal plant. A University of Michigan football coach, Tony Mason, is credited with owning the first Mackle-built home on Marco Island.

FIVE-PHASE PLAN

The island would be divided into five construction units - as the first unit was nearing completion, the company would re-apply to the U.S. Army Corps of Engineers for the permit to begin work on the next unit, a practice that allowed Deltona to commit only the money needed for a limited area at one time. The success of this arrangement was astounding, even to the Mackles and their staff, with work proceeding as fast as they could manage it.

Potential buyers here could even contract for a home sight unseen — if they later changed their mind, money would be refunded.

"It was so amazing yet in hindsight everything was so undervalued," said Leonard Llewellyn, one of Deltona's first agent/dealers. "Think about it: You could buy your own home site — $65 down and $35 a month — or you could pay cash and build right away.

"Or, we had two-, three-, four-, five- or eight-year plans . . . you'd have eight years to pay and Deltona had eight years to put in the improvements."

TOP: LEFT TO RIGHT:
HEADLINES HERALD
OPENING DAY; FIRST MODEL
HOMES ON CHESTNUT COURT;
AD PROMOTING THE ISLAND

58

A DELTONA HOTEL

Marco Beach Hotel AND VILLAS

On the Gulf at Marco Island, Florida

The $800,000, 50-room Marco Beach Hotel (today's Marriott) ushered in Opening Day with a bang. Carpet was still being laid as the first visitors arrived yet the site could not have been more alluring. Staff was all smiles and visitors were in awe of the setting. The grounds featured an inviting swimming pool plus a pitch-and-putt golf course all framed by the turquoise-blue Gulf waters and the endless beach.

Nine miles of roads were being paved, the $150,000-yacht club — the first of five planned for the area — golf course, shopping center and gas station were under construction and Marco Island's first beach front housing development, the Emerald Beach condominium, was moving along nicely. Prices started at $19,900 when it was completed in 1966, vacant beach included.

BY THE NUMBERS

The glorious plan ultimately called for 125 miles of paved roads and more than 90 miles of canals. Land was set aside for more than 12,000 home sites, 425 acres for resort hotels, 340 acres for future apartment construction, 275 acres for commercial development in planned business districts, 113 acres for schools and churches and 17 acres for medical facilities.

The master plan also called for key recreational amenities — the golf course, yachts clubs and marina facilities would be enhanced by a residents' beach club on 1,000 feet of Gulf frontage — plus an extensive system of community parks.

Deltona, in fact, left nothing to chance. Steps were taken to construct berms to reduce mosquito larvae growth, and aerial spraying also began. Since the Mackles owned offshore permits to the island, they dredged fill from the bays to raise home sites to the level required by county codes, hoping also to provide some security against storms and tidal surges. This also aided in reducing mosquito breeding areas.

The company even maintained its own repair shop on the island given Marco's remote location. The brothers did not want any form of construction to be slowed by mechanical breakdowns. As such, at the south end of the island where a former U.S. Air Force missile tracking station stood — rumored to have also been a strategic CIA eavesdropping post with Cuba just miles to the south — repairs were conducted in earnest. The same location served as headquarters for the Mackle's land development and construction operations, supplies were stored here and their own concrete produced. A fleet of concrete trucks operated daily. Today, residents of Cape Marco call the site home.

On Opening Day, visitors came by car yet waited in long lines at the only automobile access point to the island at that time: A swing bridge in Goodland. Others flew in on small, Mackle-chartered planes, landing on a dirt strip in front of the Marco Beach Hotel. Many also came by boat, like the Calusa Indians, Spanish explorers and early pioneers who carved lives here before.

TAHITI ROAD MODEL HOMES

THE SELLING OF DREAMS

Imagine, for a moment, arriving at Marco Island for Opening Day. Behind the wheel of your car or seated on a bus you would make your way across the swing bridge and ultimately along San Marco Road to the Deltona sales office. It was an impressive sight — Savage had designed this handsome building with a stone façade, two flags, fountains and a beautiful bronze sculpture of seagulls in flight.

Inside was a three-dimensional table model of the island as it would appear when completed. Large windows let the sun pour in. Nearby, the 10 model homes on Tahiti Road completely furnished and landscaped. South, on Indian Hill, the highest point on Marco at 52 feet above sea level, was a wooden observation tower for viewing the entire island. The brothers had even arranged for scenic boat trips in *The Marco Islander*, a splendid Polynesian-styled craft in keeping with the island's bold new design theme.

You could continue driving west from the sales office along San Marco to its intersection with Collier Boulevard, where Residents' Beach is today. A right turn would soon lead you to the location of Deltona's other 12 model homes, on Chestnut Court, near the elegant, Savage-designed Marco Island Yacht Club.

"What a heady time it was for all of us," said Savage. "The response to Opening Day actually took the Mackle brothers by surprise, I'm sure of it. Then, and only then, we knew we were on to something."

Several locations were available for lunch: The Yacht Club terrace, the Marco Beach Hotel or the Olde Marco Inn. Many visitors simply soaked up the sun and had picnic lunches on the sparkling beach and, just like the Mackles three years before, they too were falling in love with the place. Others, having just experienced the cold and dreary January weather up north, and in parts of Europe, were mesmerized by this enchanting little island. Hundreds signed up on the spot to purchase a Savage-built home, sold by Deltona executive Neil Bahr and his impressive sales team, in the newest and grandest of all Mackle communities.

"We were selling dreams that Opening Day so long ago," said Bahr. "Looking back at it now our sales pitches could not have been truer: There will never be another Marco Island."

RIGHT: JAN. 31, 1965
12-PAGE OPENING DAY
NEWSPAPER SUPPLEMENT

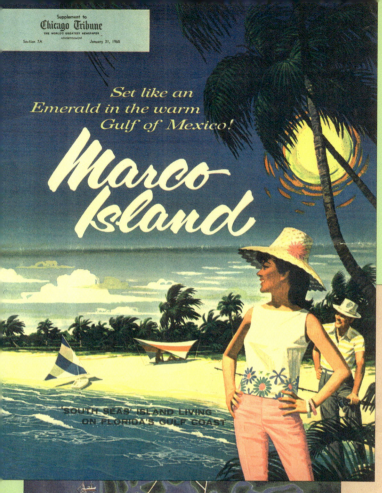

*Set like an
Emerald in the warm
Gulf of Mexico!*

Marco Island

**SOUTH SEAS' ISLAND LIVING
ON FLORIDA'S GULF COAST**

THE ISLANDER / a spacious tri-level luxury villa on the water. 3 bedrooms, 2 baths, with a double gar

Marco Island
MACKLE-BUILT VILLAS

THE MARTINIQUE / spacious waterfront with the simplicity of tropical elegance
3 bedrooms, 2 baths, powder room, screened patio, double garage and lan

A GREAT FLORIDA ADVENTURE AW
WITH TOTAL TROPICAL LIVING!

The boy becomes a man, but his boyhood dream remains unchanged — to some day
live on a lush, breeze-swept tropical island, with the enchantment of the South Seas!
Now awaken, and find that dream is real, just as Marco Island is awakening to find a
delightful seashore community of charming villas blending with its picturesque land and sea.
The Mackle brothers, Florida's renowned community builders, are opening
the last major tropical island in Florida, carefully preserving the beauty that nature
created. They are also creating a mood for living gloriously different than any you've ever kno
A swim before breakfast in the vari-colored gulf; slowly passing days in balmy breezes and sun
by tropical flora; dinner on the terrace where you're serenaded by the gentle surf — then a sa
the sunset — that's part of what living on Marco Island means! You'll also enjoy
good health in a wonderful frost-free climate. Healthy outdoor living and, above all,
days without end that are free from stress and strife. Marco Island's superb, breeze swept
sub tropical climate, with warm days and cool nights, all combine to give you a real
zest for living! The most wonderful part is that YOU can own
a charming Mackle Villa or a spacious homesite on Marco Island, and add
the flavor and pulse-tingling excitement of island living to YOUR life!

MILEAGES

Naples ...... 28 miles
Miami ...... 104 miles
Ft. Myers ...... 63 miles
Tampa ...... 189 miles

TAMPA

**MARCO ISLAND HAS ALL THE HAUNTING
ALLURE OF THE SOUTH SEAS...BUT
MARCO ISLAND IS HERE ON
FLORIDA'S GULF COAST**

the Marco Islander

SAVVY PR FUELS GROWTH

Revered primarily as quality builders, the Mackle brothers were equally adept in a public relation's capacity.

Savvy advertising campaigns coupled with a media relations moxie, the brothers spared no expense to spread the gospel of Marco. Their creative branding efforts and sales pitches catapulted the island into the consciousness of both U.S. and global consumers.

During the 1964-1965 World's Fair in New York, to tout Marco and their other Florida developments, the brothers actually built one of their homes on site. Tens of thousands of visitors toured it. The $100,000 price tag to construct the $12,000 home was as unique a publicity stunt as it was costly.

Long before today's Internet and smart phone world, print was king and the Mackles had no shortage of creative ways to make the island relevant, especially when it came to newspaper and magazine coverage.

Aside from the obvious news story angles — sprawling beaches and shiny new affordable homes under glorious sunshine in a resort/leisure community like no other — there were a host of other interesting Marco Island avenues to explore which fed the media machine.

Annual antique car shows and sailing regattas, professional men's and women's tennis tournaments and an ahead-of-its time newsletter (*The Marco Islander*) showcased all things Marco. How broad was the public relations reach? In 1971, a new ladies resort wear dubbed "The Marco Island Line" by its designers, Peck & Peck of New York, was launched at the Marco Beach Hotel during a fashion show under the auspices of *Vogue* magazine. Even Chrysler sought a piece of the co-branding pie. They unveiled their 1973 automobile line at the hotel — vehicles were actually parked pool side — far away from the not-so-balmy Detroit winter.

Of course, no new island development on Florida's rugged west coast could ever be without its folkloric mystique. By the end of 1965 Deltona chief architect Jim Vensel believed he had found evidence that a pirate ship laden with gold treasure had once foundered on the beach. So convinced was Vensel he had the company move equipment to the spot on the beach where he believed the ship had sunk. The locale was apparently some 90 feet west of Quinn's restaurant at the Marco Beach Hotel. Workers toiled for a full day and wood fragments were believed to have been found — could it have been from a pirate ship after all? — but the hunt was soon terminated. It only added to the growing legend of Marco Island and the media loved it.

THE MARCO PR MACHINE

While no single Marco Island media account would make or break the Mackle brothers, one prominent article was a sign of good things to come. The July 1964 edition of *American Builder* magazine featured a tanned Frank Jr. on its cover. Editors were impressed by the Mackles and the magazine article focused on their vision, planning and execution of the entire Marco Island project. Nothing quite like it had ever been seen, the publication said, in the annals of U.S. real estate development history.

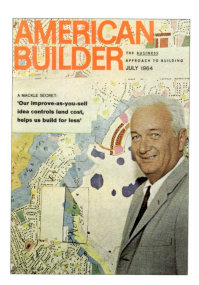

FRANK MACKLE JR.

Soon, major dailies were calling as did editorial teams at *Time* and *Forbes* magazines. Sun-starved writers and editors could not get to Marco Island soon enough to jump on America's greatest real estate story. The promise of a magical South Seas retirement, the likes few had ever dreamed possible, was a story not to be missed.

The buzz also attracted a who's who list of celebrities to the island from a host of business, literary, show business and sports fields. Complementing their paid advertising, newspaper supplements

Eugenio Saraceni, *better known as golf icon Gene Sarazen, was the first major celebrity to call Marco Island home. He and his wife Mary were also among the island's most generous philanthropists before her passing in 1986 and his in 1999 at the age of 97. The first professional to win all four of golf's major championships — the PGA, the U.S. Open, the Masters and British Open — Sarazen carded a double eagle en route to his lone Masters crown in 1935. It sealed his legend. Sarazen was instrumental in putting Marco Island on the map in the late 1960s and beyond, having chaired "the greatest one-day golf tournament in America" here for over a decade. He capped his illustrious career with a hole-in-one during his final professional tournament appearance — it was the 1973 British Open no less — at the age of 71. Inventor of the sand wedge, Sarazen affectionately dubbed "The Squire" for his always impeccable attire, was inducted into the World Golf Hall of Fame in 1974 and when the PGA Tour inaugurated its Lifetime Achievement Award in 1996 Sarazen was the first recipient.*

and radio spots globally would now be a plethora of free publicity as Marco slowly became the new *"it"* place to see and be seen. Hugely popular television host, *The Tonight Show's* Jack Paar, even cut a promotional video extolling the virtues of the Mackle-built haven. Paar gushed with unbridled enthusiasm.

Building great bricks-and-mortar also helped the cause. The Marco Beach Hotel and the Marco Island Country Club, which opened in February 1966, would prove to be an invaluable one-two punch in their ultimate media-driven quest to raise island awareness and to propel home and lot sales.

THE WHO'S WHO LIST

Golf legend Gene Sarazen was the first big name to call Marco home. By 1966, he found himself sharing it with Marco Island Country Club touring pro "Champagne" Tony Lema and a host of others. U.S. Senator George Smathers, C.L. Woody, executive vice-president of National Airlines, Marshall Smith, senior editor of *Life* magazine, plus athletes, civic and business leaders and media giants had each made their way south. Before the year was out, future President Richard Nixon, Hobart Lewis, president of *Reader's Digest*, Purdue University football coach Jack Mollenkopf and Cleveland Browns football coach Blanton Collier had been visitors here. The Mackles could not have asked for a more diverse group of high profile individuals to spend time at the hotel and on the links. The publicity was golden.

Sadly, however, Lema's time would be cut short. By the summer of 1966 the popular golfer and his wife Betty were dead. The couple died in an airplane crash following a PGA event in Akron, Ohio. He was just 32 and at the peak of his success. Devastated, yet in tribute, the Mackles hosted a memorial golf tournament in his honor for well over a decade and, while deeply mourning the loss, it became a hugely successful yearly ritual attracting some of the world's top golfers and celebrities. Early on, Sarazen was joined by entertainment icon Ed Sullivan — they were best friends growing up as caddies back in 1912 at the Apawamis Club in Rye,

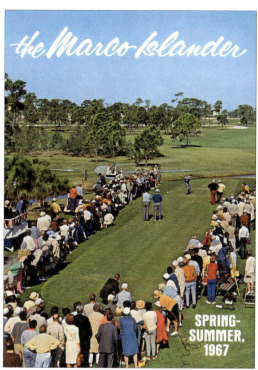

the Marco Islander

SPRING-SUMMER, 1967

TOP: LEMA TOURNAMENT ATTENDEES OVER THE YEARS INCLUDED (FROM LEFT, TOP ROW) RICHARD NIXON, TEEING OFF; JOE NAMATH; JOE DIMAGGIO, JOE GARAGIOLA AND YOGI BERRA; STAN MUSIAL AND JOE DIMAGGIO; PERRY COMO WITH GENE SARAZEN; SARAZEN, ROBERT MACKLE, REV. BILLY GRAHAM AND LEMA PARTICIPANT; TERRY BRADSHAW AND BOB GRIESE

New York — and Nixon as tournament co-chairs. The triumvirate was so successful pulling big names to Marco that the Lema outing became known as "the greatest one-day golf tournament in America." If you were one of the lucky few to be in the tournament's orbit it was not to be missed. The free publicity from such mega-watt star power proved time and time again to be a public relation's coup although the Mackle brothers never lost sight of the fact that such enormous recognition for the island was the result of the loss of their talented friend.

With such star power fuelling the publicity engine, there was no better time to be in the real estate field. Marco Island was a ground-floor opportunity like no other. No sooner had Deltona promotional materials dropped across the nation, and abroad, the feedback from potential customers was immediate. Over the years Deltona expanded its sales force to include 157 dealers to spread the news, including 27 in foreign countries. Most of the initial U.S. sales thrust was centered in the Midwest and Northeastern markets. The dynamic PR push was so polished and successful, Deltona sales figures revealed that a whopping 90 percent of their customers bought home sites here *sight unseen*.

Others, of course, made the pilgrimage to Marco to see what all the fuss was about. As such, Deltona hurriedly expanded the Marco Beach Hotel

from 50 to 100 rooms in 1967, complete with shuffleboard, its pitch-and-putt golf course, pool and other amenities including 12 spacious villas. The addition, while welcomed, proved to be another stroke of genius as it continued to sell out.

By 1968, the island population had grown to an estimated 1,000 residents and Deltona was continually adding new home models to the market plus expanding their Marco Island and vicinity empire. They purchased the north half of neighboring Kice Island, which included two and a half miles of new beach front rivaling Marco in its beauty. In 1969 and in early 1970 another 9,040 acres of nearby land was acquired bringing the total ownership of land on or near Marco to almost 20,000 acres, including Horr's Island (today's Key Marco), acreage south of Marco and east of Kice Island.

STAGGERING PROGRESS

Nearing the island's fifth birthday, progress was staggering.

Over 500 apartment units had been completed and another 172 were under construction. The first beachfront condominiums — Emerald Beach (completed in 1966 and at seven stories the tallest building on

"Champagne" Tony Lema, right, had been touring pro of the Marco Island Country Club for just one year, the first and only private club post in his professional career, when he and his wife Betty died on July 24, 1966 in a plane crash following a PGA Tour event in Akron, Ohio. He was 32 years old and at the peak of his success having won over $100,000 in prize money in 1964 and 1965. "Champagne" Tony, whose nickname dated back to 1962 when he asked the press to help him celebrate a tournament victory with a case of champagne, had been on the PGA tour since 1957. His biggest victory occurred in 1964, when he captured his first and only major: The British Open. Marco developers Elliott, Robert and Frank Mackle Jr., along with golf icon Gene Sarazen, each played pivotal roles in attracting Lema to the Marco post. After his death, the brothers and Sarazen rolled up their sleeves to honor their friend. The Tony Lema Memorial Golf Tournament attracted top celebrities and athletes to Marco for over a decade and became known quite simply as "the greatest one-day golf tournament in America."

Lema is shown with, from left, Sarazen and Frank Mackle Jr.

Marco at the time), Sunset House (1969) and Sunset House North (1970) offered a host of conveniences plus awe-inspiring sunsets daily.

The $800,000 Marco Town Center opened in 1969, the island's first drug store appeared and a medical clinic was in operation.

The sole law enforcement officer on the island, Les Binns, was authorized to hire two deputies, and by the end of the year, Marco's first fire station had opened.

Celebrities continued to flock to the island — model/actress Victoria Principal and baseball greats Mickey Mantle and Stan Musial spent time here — as the 1960s came to a close. Young local residents started making an impact as well. Two friends, Jimmy Brawner and Ivan Burley, began Marco's first Boy Scout troop and Lynne Topping, a former pool manager at the Marco Beach Hotel, was named Miss Florida 1969.

Over 9,500 home sites had been sold and recreational facilities were under construction. A new toll bridge spanned the Marco River — the Marco Pass Bridge (later named the Judge S. S. Jolley Bridge) — opened on Dec. 13, 1969. Topping was present. She had the honor of breaking a ceremonial champagne bottle against the concrete span.

Marco Island's first bank opened in 1970. Prices for a two-bedroom home now started at $29,800 while four-bedroom waterfront models began at $53,700.

Financing Problems Settled

Way Cleared For Marco Island Bridge

ABOVE: MARCO MODEL HOMES; NEW MARCO BRIDGE TO BECOME A REALITY

CBS television launched a special on the world's top fishing spots and included Marco in its broadcast. Rev. Billy Graham, football heroes Joe Namath and Johnny Unitas were among those who participated in the fourth annual Lema Memorial Golf Tournament. Astronaut James Lovell visited and pro Lee Trevino was photographed here for a book about golf.

THE BIG GAMBLE

The boldest bricks-and-mortar move ever undertaken by the Mackles occurred on Dec. 18, 1971, when they altered Marco Island's beach skyline forever. The Marco Beach Hotel & Villas (today's Marriott) expanded yet again and now included one of its two present-day towers.

It was an $18-million gamble. Designed by Deltona architect Herb Savage, the new structure was a 10-storey, 400-room masterpiece, all with Gulf views and rivaling that of any similar resort on the planet. Savage won an impressive international award for it.

Like so many Mackle projects, the hands-on attention to detail left nothing to chance. So driven was Frank Jr., he actually ordered a mock guest room to be built on the parking lot at Deltona's Miami headquarters.

The hotel's entrance, somewhat surprising to some, was actually on the second floor. "My father wanted it that way," said Frank Mackle III. "Upon entering the wide wood-and-glass doors to the lobby, he wanted the guests elevated to see — through three stories of glass — an enormous pool, the blue-green waters of the Gulf of Mexico and the eye-squinting white Gulf beach all framed by tropical lawns and landscaping. If a party was to arrive a few moments before the end of the day they were spellbound by the brilliant red and orange and yellow sunsets."

Standard rooms were also much larger than those in similar high-class Florida resorts at the time.

The Marco Islander, Deltona's color newsletter distributed far and wide, summed up the hotel's grand opening:

The formal dedication and official opening of the new Marco Beach Hotel combined just the right mixture of ceremony and carnival; it was easily the most momentous of all grand openings since the Mackle built community was launched seven years ago.

On a sunny and warm Saturday afternoon, several hundred guests gathered in the expansive lobby of the new resort complex to formally dedicate the striking edifice which rises 10 stories above a crescent-shaped three-mile beach.

RIGHT: THE MARCO BEACH HOTEL & VILLAS (TODAY'S MARRIOTT) THROUGH THE YEARS: LOOKING NORTH, 1968 (NOTE THE EMERALD BEACH CONDOMINIUM OFF IN THE DISTANCE); TOWER CONSTRUCTION, 1970; ROBERT AND FRANK JR. BEAMING WHEN THE TOWER OPENED IN 1971.

"We wanted a hotel that would be unique to this island and that would be in keeping with all of the natural beauties that surround us," said Deltona president Frank Mackle Jr.

Honored guest, Florida Governor Reubin Askew, complimented the Mackles on the new hotel. Hors d'oeuvres were served and champagne receptions were held around the hexagonal swimming pool, in its restaurants and in the convention center's meeting rooms. A gourmet-style pool-side cocktail party followed. A lavish banquet concluded the day's festivities in the richly appointed Promenade ballroom where 1,000 guests were entertained by two orchestras and vocalist Jaye P. Morgan.

Goodyear Blimp Mayflower circled the hotel while flashing congratulations and welcoming messages to hotel guests many of whom took advantage of Goodyear's invitation to enjoy half-hour aerial tours over the island. Golf and tennis tournaments and a fashion show presented with the assistance of the editorial staff of Vogue magazine followed.

Guests took advantage of the near-perfect weather to sun beside the pool or on the soft sand beach. The luxury resort's fleet of sailboats, bicycles, and motor bikes was in continuous use.

Quinn's, the hotel's version of Tahiti's famous waterfront bistro, was the site of a Sunday evening cocktail party and luau.

The official opening concluded with Monday morning breakfasts in two of the hotel's dining rooms and at noon the newest and largest hotel on the Gulf of Mexico opened to the public.

Frank Jr. dedicated the hotel to his wife, Virginia — the ceremony actually fell on her birthday no less — and he dubbed the property "The Jewel of the Gulf."

The publicity was monumental and it wasn't long before major companies and organizations were planning conventions and business meetings on Marco as the Mackle brothers had anticipated all along.

"It was Dad's dream to build a world-class resort that would transform Marco into a convention and tourist destination," said Frank Mackle III.

How important was this hotel to the growth of Marco? Deltona records reveal that in the first year after the hotel opened, Marco condominium sales revenue nearly tripled from $4.5 million in 1971 to $12.4 million in 1972.

The launch of the new hotel may very well have been the Mackle brothers finest hour. In fact, reflecting back on this time, Frank Mackle III said the hotel unveiling represented "the pinnacle" of his father's many achievements.

Storm clouds, however, were brewing. The memory of the launch and the sheer joy of accomplishment for the brothers would soon take a back seat to factors beyond their control that would change Marco Island — and their lives — forever.

TOP LEFT: A FESTIVE OPENING DAY WEEKEND USHERED IN THE NEW MARCO BEACH HOTEL & VILLAS IN DECEMBER, 1971.

ONWARD AND UPWARD

Nevertheless, it was full steam ahead. Shortly after the hotel's unveiling, Deltona formed Marco Island Airways early in 1972. The carrier flew five round trips daily between Marco and Miami. Prior to 1972, planes landed on present-day Landmark Street, just a stone's throw from the beach. Later, when Landmark was developed, planes simply landed on the island's second airstrip, near present-day Edgewater and Bonita courts. The late Gil Nordell, one of the first Marco Beach Hotel employees who would go on to spend a 40-year career at the property/Marriott, often flicked his car headlights on and off while seated in a Mackle vehicle to actually guide planes at dusk to their destination. The brothers never flew together for obvious reasons. Nordell would pick up two brothers and drop them off at the hotel entrance before returning to the dirt airstrip, flashing his car lights once again, to guide the next plane to a safe landing where a third brother would emerge.

Admiralty House, a 200-unit condominium on the beach was completed in 1972 and rose 18 stories above the Gulf. Tradewinds, the fifth condominium located at the north end of the beach, opened in 1973, as did the 265-unit Gulfview Club, at 21 stories the tallest building on Marco at the time. It towered above Residents' Beach. Later, Summit House in 1981 and Royal Seafarer in 1982 would, at 22 stories apiece, eclipse Gulfview.

By the end of 1973, the population had jumped to an estimated 5,000 full- and part-time residents. More than 700 single-family homes and 1,500 condominium units had been completed.

Former baseball catcher and broadcaster Joe Garagiola purchased a condominium in 1974 and joked, "Now Gene Sarazen will have to share his island with me." Over the next few years, football's Bob Griese, golfers Arnold Palmer and Jack Nicklaus and astronaut Jack Swigert were among the visitors, further fueling the concept that Marco was the "it" place to be.

FRANKLY SPEAKING

When the modern era's 10th birthday arrived, in 1975, Frank Jr. was glowing but not so much because of bricks-and-mortar milestones, rather, he beamed because Marco Island was home to great people who sought to live here.

"Since our Opening Day in 1965, hundreds of thousands of people have come to witness the orderly conversion/growth of this unique island into a showcase community of spacious and splendid homes, impressive high-rise condominiums, garden-type apartments, a wide range of recreational facilities, shopping centers, churches, and the largest resort hotel complex on the Gulf of Mexico," he said.

"The transition in the past decade has been spectacular in many respects. More than $150 million has been spent by the Deltona Corporation on building and land development at Marco since its unveiling. Home sites have totaled more than $168 million and home and apartment sales have exceeded $83 million.

"But, what really makes Marco a special place in my mind is the emergence of a fine community spirit. Marco has a character all its own and the people who live here appreciate that. I think this is reflected in the pride of ownership that exists. Marco residents think their community is number one . . . and, they should!"

By the mid-1970s a second bridge connected the island with the mainland at Goodland, twin theaters were operating on Elkcam Circle ("Elkcam" is "Mackle" spelled backwards), and the present-day, off-island home of the Marco Island Executive Airport was completed near the Marco Shores development on Mainsail Drive

From 1975 to 1980, three new shopping centers, a variety of restaurants, two banks and two savings and loan associations, a post office, three churches and the island's first 24-hour ambulance and rescue service were operational. Hideaway Beach Club, a private, gated community featuring a clubhouse, golf course and tennis facilities where Marco's founder made landfall in 1870, was on the drawing boards.

ABOVE: LONG TIME MARCO BEACH HOTEL/MARRIOTT EMPLOYEE GIL NORDELL, LEFT, ISLAND ARCHITECT HERB SAVAGE AND DELTONA'S FRANK MACKLE III, SHARE A MOMENT IN 2008

TOP LEFT TO RIGHT: MARCO ISLAND AIRWAYS MARCO ISLAND COUNTRY CLUB

With 1980 around the corner, the Marco Island Area Chamber of Commerce, which incorporated in 1977, had grown to 180 members representing 95 percent of all island business. The population had increased to an estimated 6,000 full- and part-time residents, 7,000 developed home sites, 772 single-family homes and more than 1,900 condominium apartments had been completed. Two major developments with gorgeous views at opposite ends of the island were soon finished. The four-tower South Seas beach complex and its 1,264 units at the island's northwestern end, begun in 1976, was completed in 1982. Shipp's Landing, 206 units on waterfront property at the southeastern end of the island, begun in 1979, was completed in 1985.

Behind the scenes, however, it could not have been more difficult for the brothers. Building a paradise for others to enjoy would cost them dearly, in health and personal treasure. It certainly didn't start that way but it would end terribly for them.

The trio with the Midas touch, who easily maneuvered the marketing and public relations landscape, would now be in the news for all the wrong reasons. Agonizing and unprecedented court battles, based on their desire to build on environmentally sensitive land, would drag on for over a decade and bring an avalanche of negative publicity. Combined, it would seal their doom,

The Mackle brothers' vision for Marco Island would soon be coming to an end.

ABOVE: CHRYSLER UNVEILED ITS 1973 AUTOMOBILE LINE AT THE MARCO BEACH HOTEL & VILLAS; THE SWING BRIDGE TO GOODLAND/MARCO WOULD BE NO MORE AS CONSTRUCTION ON A NEW SPAN WAS UNDERWAY IN THE EARLY 1970s
NEXT PAGE: MARCO ISLAND PROGRESS, 1973 & 2013

THE CURSE. THE KIDNAPPING. THE CORPS.

If the Mackle brothers believed they were the first to witness the island's potential, they would sorely have been mistaken. Marco was a graveyard of broken development dreams before they arrived on the scene, regardless of era, and its rugged beauty nothing more than a cruel façade since its founding in 1870.

Just about anyone who tried to build on sacred Calusa Indian ground here, it seemed, failed miserably or suffered unspeakable tragedy.

Did a curse really exist?

EARLY PIONEER ANGUISH

W.D. Capt. Bill Collier, the son of the island's founder, was particularly doomed.

He was the first entrepreneur on sacred Calusa land at the north end of the island. A farmer, boatbuilder, storeowner and hotel operator based in Marco village (today's Olde Marco), Capt. Bill suffered beyond compare. He lost his mother (she burned to death on the island after her clothing caught fire); 16-year-old daughter Agnes, in a separate island fire; 23-year-old brother Benjamin drowned after falling overboard on a sailing trip; plus his first wife died giving birth to a stillborn child. If that wasn't enough for anyone to endure, further heartache soon followed Capt. Bill at the turn of the 20th Century when, on another sailing trip, he watched in horror as his three young sons — plus six members of a visiting Connecticut family — all drowned when his boat capsized in a storm off the Florida Keys. Sons George (8 years old), Thomas (6), and Wilmer (4) were the first residents to be buried in the Marco Island Cemetery.

At the same time, men, women *and* children would work here for pennies in clam factories located directly on Calusa ground. The J. Harvey Doxsee clam cannery in Marco village and the Elmer S. Burnham plant five miles south in Caxambas were prolific, prompting the arrival of the Atlantic Coast Line Railway to transport clam products to market. But within a few short decades, the factories and the railroad went bust because the clams were gone.

In the early 1920s husband and wife pioneers James and Tommie Barfield saw gold via land development in Caxambas. They subdivided their holdings, pitched glorious waterfront views and despite just $200 for each lot, failed to sell a single one. Their biggest blow, however, occurred on Christmas Eve 1932, when their youngest daughter Ava died in an automobile accident. She was 22.

By the late 1920s a New York-based syndicate that included the powerful Ruppert family, owners of breweries and the New York Yankees baseball club, acquired Capt. Bill's land with big dreams for Marco village. They could not make a go of it, however, as their 525 subdivided lots stood still — and unsold — as The Crash of 1929 and the subsequent Great Depression took hold.

BARRON'S DEMISE

Not even the most powerful, deep-pocketed man of the era, New York street-car advertising tycoon Barron Gift Collier (no relation to Capt. Bill), could make a go of it here. Collier purchased one million acres of Southwest Florida real estate in the 1920s — including 90 per cent of Marco Island — but his incredibly ambitious development plans on Calusa land at Caxambas never got off the ground.

Barron drew plans for a major sea port, yacht basins, horse racing track, golf course, residential homes and a large lumber mill. To further facilitate the development, the state incorporated Marco as Collier City in 1927, named not for Barron but W.T. Collier, the island's founder.

Collier City, of course, never materialized. The Great Depression followed and Barron's wealth depleted considerably. Within a decade, Barron would die just 10 days shy of his 66th birthday in 1939.

Two of his three heirs would meet untimely deaths.

Sons Barron Jr., Sam and Miles moved homes from Caxambas in 1949, and the families who lived in them, to neighboring Goodland to make way for their own development plans. Sam, however, died in a 1950 auto racing accident at Watkins Glen in New York and Miles, in 1954, succumbed to polio. Each brother did not live long enough to reach his 40th birthday.

Ill himself, Barron Jr. didn't have the resolve to tackle Marco alone. As such, he and his advisors attempted to wash themselves of the island completely. They tried to sell it to the State of Florida as a nature preserve. The state, however, turned them down. The $1-million price tag was simply too costly.

With the 1960s now upon them, Barron Jr. and his team reached out to a group of reputable Miami-based developers. The Mackle brothers — Elliott, Robert and Frank Jr. — fell in love with the island the minute they arrived on its unspoiled beach in 1962. It wasn't long before an amicable deal was reached. The three brothers would own virtually all of Marco Island for $7 million.

MACKLE DAUGHTER BURIED ALIVE

While the brothers would go on to make the greatest impact of any developers, before or since, they too were not immune to setbacks or devastating heartache.

In 1968, as a global marketing campaign to sell Marco Island to the world was in full swing and bringing unprecedented attention to it — and the Mackles — the buzz attracted more than just potential new home owners.

LEFT: BARRON COLLIER'S HEIRS, SAM, MILES AND BARRON JR., WITH TAMIAMI TRAIL ENGINEER DAVID GRAHAM COPELAND

TOP RIGHT: BARBARA JANE MACKLE, SEDATED, INSIDE A CAPSULE AND THE PLOT WHERE SHE WAS BURIED ALIVE

The nation was shocked to learn that Barbara Jane Mackle, Robert's 20-year-old daughter and a student at Emory University, had been kidnapped in Georgia just before Christmas.

She was buried alive in a crude box for 83 hours. Kidnappers demanded a $500,000 ransom from Robert. With poor ventilation, and the water she drank spiked with a sedative, frightened Barbara clung to a note handed to her by her captors. In part it read:

Do not be alarmed. You are safe. You are presently inside a fiberglass reinforced plywood capsule buried beneath the ground near the house in which your kidnappers are staying. Your status will be checked approximately every 2 hours.

The capsule is quite strong. You will not be able to break it open. Be advised, however, that you are beneath the water table. If you break open a seam you would drown before we could dig you out . . .

Your life depends on the air delivered to your chamber via the ventilation fan . . . if we detect any commotion which we feel is dangerous, we will introduce ether to the air intake and put you to sleep . . .

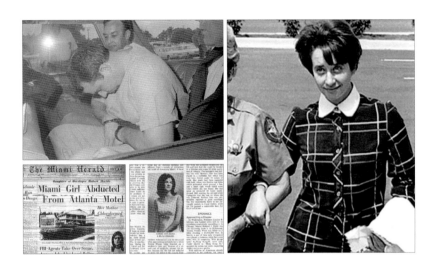

The ventilation system is doubly screened to prevent insects or animals from entering the capsule area. You risk being eaten by ants should you break these protection screens. The electrical components behind these screens are delicate and they support your life. Don't attempt to touch these circuits . . .

We're sure your father will pay the ransom we have asked in less than one week. When your father pays the ransom we will tell him where you are and he'll come for you. Should he fail to pay we will release you, so be calm and rest – you'll be home for Christmas one way or the other.

Deeply distraught, Robert hurriedly walked into his Miami bank branch and quietly requested the ransom amount in small bills. Incredibly, he did not have to put up collateral to secure it. His word was good enough.

The FBI cracked the case three-and-a-half days later when they found a dehydrated Barbara buried underground in the capsule, yet still alive, some 30 miles north of Atlanta in a forested area. Agents calmly spoke to her as they frantically removed the dirt. Barbara pleaded with them not to leave. She was reunited with her family in time for Christmas.

Her abductors were apprehended and arrested for the kidnapping. Gary Steven Krist and his accomplice, Ruth Eisemann-Schier, were later convicted of the charges. While Krist was picked up almost immediately, Schier remained on the run for 79 days after the kidnapping and holds the dubious distinction of being the first woman named to the FBI's 10 Most Wanted list. A Honduran national, she was later deported from the United States after serving just four years of a seven-year sentence. Krist received a life sentence but only served 10 years in prison before he was released. He wrote a book about the experience in 1972: *Life: The Man Who Kidnapped Barbara Jane Mackle.* He would go on to become a medical doctor in rural Indiana before his credentials were revoked in 2003 — he apparently lied about disciplinary action received during his residency. Most recently he was back in prison on drug smuggling charges.

Barbara has shunned the spotlight for decades, refusing all media requests to speak about her ordeal. She did collaborate, however, on a book with late two-time Pulitzer Prize-winning *Miami Herald* journalist Gene Miller shortly after the kidnapping. *83 Hours 'Til Dawn* was published in 1971. Two made-for-television movies, *The Longest Night* and *83 Hours 'Til Dawn*, soon followed.

Robert, the go-to, no-nonsense Mackle brother when it came to finances and dealing with union issues on job sites across the State of Florida, would never be the same.

THE MARCH TO RUIN

The Marco development, meanwhile, still in its infancy and full of promise when Barbara returned home safely, was on a path to ruin but none of the brothers saw it coming.

As Mackle bulldozers and heavy equipment began shaping the first of five development phases — it had taken all of six months to secure the necessary county, state and federal dredge-and-fill permits — the unthinkable happened. The U.S. Army Corps of Engineers, which

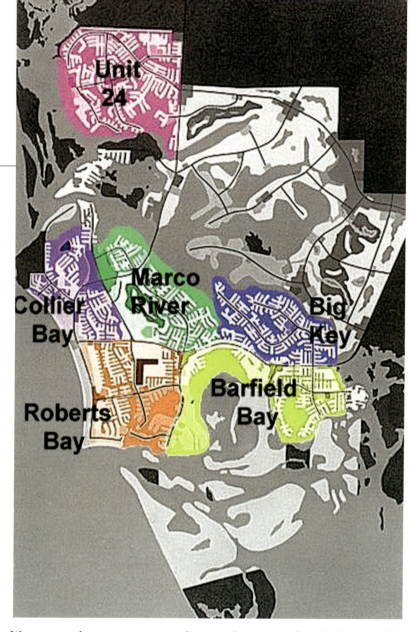

initially took but nine days to approve Marco's first dredge-and-fill permit, took two years to approve permits for the second phase.

It was now the early 1970s and the dawn of a new anti-development era was upon them. The Mackle brothers would become the pawns in a costly power struggle between governments and the fledgling environmental and conservation movements which bitterly waged war against them to preserve Marco's fragile wetlands and natural habitat.

The newly formed Collier County Conservancy would ultimately join forces with the Environmental Defense Fund, the Sierra Club, Audubon Society and Nature Conservancy, among others, in an all-out, no-holds-barred battle to block the Marco development.

"It was the first big street fight where the greens got a real victory. Before that, we had been written off as a joke. Marco Island put us on the map," said David Guest, head of the Florida Regional Office of EarthJustice, in a 2012 interview with the Reuters news agency.

Adding to Deltona's woes, additional environmental responsibilities had been granted to the Corps *after* the Marco project had begun. Plus, a series of new state and federal environmental protection laws soon followed as did a growing government bureaucracy that also included the newly minted Environmental Protection Agency (EPA) at the federal level in 1970.

RIGHT: MARCO ISLAND'S FIVE- PHASE DEVELOPMENT PLAN PLUS UNIT 24

It wasn't long before various agencies were at odds with each other over the complexities of environmental jurisdiction and the very interpretation of the growing new regulations each was charged to uphold. It was a lawyer's dream but an absolute nightmare for the brothers. The lawsuits and court challenges — one after another — would drag on between Deltona, governments and environmental groups for over a decade.

"The rules changed in the middle of the game," lamented Deltona sales chief Neil Bahr. "We planned meticulously. We were given the green light and . . . then . . . everything slowed to a crawl before stopping altogether.

We were caught up in a never-ending regulatory mess for which we would never recover."

In an effort to appease all sides, in 1972, Deltona agreed to deed 4,000 acres of real estate to the State of Florida. It would stay pristine forever. In return, the state would do its part to move the Marco development forward.

Meanwhile, perturbed by the delays yet confident they would ultimately prevail at the federal level, the Mackles directed Bahr and his prolific

sales team to continue selling lots on nearby acreage where mangroves sprouted skyward from the wetlands. Buyers by the thousands confidently put money down on a true piece of Florida swamp land — lots were actually under water — knowing the reputable brothers would magically transform it with their dredge-and-fill expertise.

MARCO PLANS DENIED

That was the plan until April 16, 1976, when the Corps, pressured heavily by the environmentalists, denied the final two phases of the dredge-and-fill operation. It would affect some 2,100 acres of mangroves and more than 4,300 already-plotted home sites.

It was the first time in history that the government had denied a private property holder the right to fill coastal wetlands. *National Geographic* and other publications hailed the Corps decision at the time as "landmark" and "precedent-setting." No coastal wetlands in the U.S. have been filled since.

It was a devastating blow to the brothers and their company. Deltona stock plunged 28 per cent virtually overnight.

"I am shocked and outraged at the injustice of the decision, denying two of the Marco Island permits," said Frank Jr. in a company press release. "Deltona over the years has received all necessary county and state approvals for these permit areas.

"Over the past 12 years, the Marco Island development has been subjected to over 50 public hearings and has received approvals from all elected bodies that have considered our applications. All environmental and public interest issues were considered and approved in 1972 when we agreed with the highest elected officials of the State of Florida to deed over 4,000 acres to the state to be held in its natural condition.

"I am appalled that the carefully considered decisions of elected officials, made under the full glare of public scrutiny, have been overturned by the Corps bureaucracy at the Washington level."

Overshadowed by the denial was the Corps decision to approve phase three of the Deltona plan, some 1,000 acres in the Collier Bay area where 1,400 home sites would ultimately emerge.

The buildup to the Corps decision had taken a huge toll on the relationship between Robert and Frank Jr., especially. Elliott had retired in 1970 but a battle-weary Robert and a determined Frank Jr. were no longer seeing eye to eye as the company continued to bleed from its ongoing court battles. Still, Frank Jr. was convinced that justice would ultimately prevail. It would just take a little more time to reverse the Corps decision, he reasoned, and more money — lots of it — even if he had to take the case all the way to the Supreme Court of the United States.

One month after the Corps decision, Deltona filed suit in U.S. District Court in Miami challenging the denial.

"I believe the Corps decision was based upon factors unrelated to the merits of our permit applications," said Frank Jr. in a company press release. "I am confident that we will be successful in reversing the Corps decision and in obtaining the permits needed to complete Marco Island."

In a move that purely spoke to his optimism, Frank Jr. was back on the stump promoting two new beachfront hotels within 60 days of the Corps decision. He was desperate to see Deltona back in the news in a positive light and dead serious about the resort properties moving forward. Each hotel would have featured 200 rooms, one a luxury brand, the other a more affordable property for the masses. The high-end resort would have been magnificent even by Frank's standards. Situated at the south end of the beach, where today's Cape Marco stands, the hotel would have featured a 360-degree rotating restaurant on the roof. Diners would have enjoyed a panoramic landscape unlike any other on the planet: The Ten Thousand Islands to the south, the pearly white crescent-shaped beach stretching to the north plus Marco Island's remarkable sunsets ushering in happy hour and the promising evening ahead.

It was not meant to be, of course, and Robert had had enough. Less than 10 months after the Corps decision, at the age of 65, he abruptly retired

ABOVE: LEFT TO RIGHT, DELTONA'S PLIGHT

from the very entity he so proudly created with his brothers. It would later be revealed that he and Frank Jr. were not even on speaking terms near the end.

To raise funds for Deltona's mounting court battles — the crush of legal woes would actually push the company to the brink of bankruptcy — Frank Jr. turned to sales chief Bahr to sell many undeveloped Marco Island properties. Time was not on Deltona's side. Bahr, a trusted senior executive, did so at bargain basement prices and he began selling assets including the Marco Beach Hotel & Villas, Frank Jr.'s prized possession. The hotel was sold to Marriott in 1979 for $35 million.

"It was the most agonizing time of my entire career," said Bahr. "And, easily, the saddest."

THE DREAM DIES

On March 22, 1982, the larger-than-life Mackle plan for Florida's final frontier was, for all intents and purposes, over. The Supreme Court refused a Deltona petition to overturn the Corps decision. The prized permits for Big Key and Barfield Bay — the final two phases of Deltona's master plan — would not be issued. Ever. A tract of land dubbed Unit 24, off island and earmarked for future development, was also essentially wiped out by the Corps decision.

Frank Jr. took the news especially hard having believed all along that he, his brothers and their company had always acted responsibly and in good faith. Always.

Now, however, some 7,000 customers had contracts for home sites on land that could not be developed and Deltona had used much of the down payment cash flow to build island homes and costly area infrastructure. They were also saddled with a mountain of legal bills. Still, Frank Jr. insisted on meeting his company's contractual obligations and he offered cash refunds, alternative island property or exchanges for home sites in other Deltona communities while advisors encouraged him to walk away, declare bankruptcy, and begin anew.

"The stockholders of Deltona would have been better off," said Frank Jr. "But we thought the customer came first . . . all of these people who purchased from us would have been wiped out. Florida had this horrible reputation for land scams. I just decided that people would either get property or get their money back."

Added Frank III, a senior Deltona executive in his own right: "We were determined to avoid (bankruptcy) at all costs. The fact is that a bankruptcy filing which left the creditor (us) in control might have been a financially better course but the loser in such a proceeding would have been our customers, our banking relationships and, candidly, our reputation. Although we were forced to the brink several times, we were successful in avoiding that alternative."

Company records reveal that two-thirds of all home site owners requested refunds. Frank Jr. kept his word and met the challenges head on. It cost the company tens of millions of dollars and it would leave Deltona in ruins. When the dust finally settled, Deltona virtually turned all of its undeveloped holdings, thousands of acres, into nature preserves.

The totality of the Mackle vision for Marco Island? No more than a mirage. The improbable dream? Shattered.

Perhaps there really was a Calusa Indian curse after all.

A COSTLY RUN

The years of litigation, compromise, delays, public meetings, hearings, setbacks and cash refunds not only prevented the Marco project from soaring, as first imagined, but the loss of personal treasure for the Mackles from such ongoing battles may well have exceeded $100 million.

"It hurts when I think of what we could have done," said Frank Jr., in an interview with the *Marco Island Eagle* in 1990.

"Everything was computed as if we would get all the permits. Then we had to sell the (Gulf) front property. All the things we were dreaming about were crushed (by the Corps decision). We thought that it was very unfair and it's hard not to be bitter about it."

Gone, too, was the special bond between the brothers as the Marco development progressed. They owned a stable of horses and Frank Jr. enjoyed his time on the golf course but these pursuits served only as mild diversions from the Marco woes that consumed them virtually from the outset.

Some have even suggested that the legal and financial pressures alone resulted in the relatively early deaths of Elliott and Robert. Elliott passed on in 1978 at the age of 69. Robert died in 1983, shortly after the Supreme Court refused his company's petition to overturn the Corps decision. He was 71. Frank Jr., for whom the island's Mackle Park is named, died in 1993. He was 77.

It would fall on others to build the rest of Marco Island through present day although the grandiose size and scope as originally planned would never materialize.

Still, shortly before his death, the ever-optimistic Frank Jr. said he had no regrets. That fateful 1962 Marco Island beach walk with his brothers, Bahr and chief architect Jim Vensel, was the most amazing moment of his professional career.

The building of Marco Island for better or worse — curses or otherwise — would be his destiny.

"I couldn't believe Marco Island the first time I saw it," he said. "It was so beautiful. I decided right on the spot to turn Marco into a paradise everyone could enjoy."

ABOVE: FRANK MACKLE JR., NEIL BAHR AND ROBERT MACKLE IN HAPPIER TIMES.

RIGHT: DELTONA'S WOES PLAYED OUT IN THE MEDIA; INSET, THE MISSILE TRACKING STATION AT THE SOUTH END OF THE BEACH WOULD HAVE BEEN DEMOLISHED TO MAKE WAY FOR A SPECTACULAR HOTEL. IT WAS NOT MEANT TO BE. CAPE MARCO STANDS THERE TODAY.

POST-MACKLE ERA

Many dates constitute milestones and turning points for Marco Island but perhaps none more significant in the post-Mackle era than August 28, 1997.

That was the day Marco Islanders, albeit by just 181 votes, finally decided to switch from an unincorporated entity to cityhood. The last time a move like this occurred here was in the late 1920s. Marco Island was actually named Collier City for a brief period of time but it would fade quickly, however, as the looming Great Depression scuttled any hopes of progress.

The main battle cry of proponents prior to the modern-day switch had been that the county (Collier) regarded Marco as a "cash cow" (taxes and impact fees) while opponents feared that another layer of government would lead to a typically top-heavy bureaucracy.

The jury may still be out, but not since the Mackle brothers has the island had such a permanent guiding hand to lead its future.

CONDO BOOM

Those who come here do so not because of government. They arrive captivated, of course, by Marco's physical beauty. Sure, the streets are clean, plazas and malls are functional, and the handful of resort hotels are world-class but the real pull is the beach and the water. Hence, waterfront views (as well as bay and river views) have become the magnets.

So, coinciding with cityhood but not necessarily because of it, the island has experienced some profound post-Mackle era developments, two of which were a battery of beautiful high-rise condominium buildings - Belize, Cozumel, Merida, Monterrey, Tampico and Vera Cruz collectively known as Cape Marco at the south end of the beach — and a mixed-use complex on Smokehouse Bay called The Esplanade.

Integrally as well as intrinsically involved with the projects was Naples developer and businessman Jack Antaramian, lauded by some for his visionary ideas, and reviled by others who cried exploitation and overdevelopment.

But there was no denying the value of his contributions to the city skyline. The feeling, locally, was that he was a kind of da Vinci who used Marco as his palate.

Ditto in most Islanders' minds The Esplanade, which had hitherto been an ugly, flat expanse of land opposite the Winn-Dixie store on Collier Boulevard, but from which Antaramian conjured up a Mediterranean-style complex that included expensive condos, high-end shops, a marina and a slew of fairly up-market "resort casual" restaurants.

The Esplanade's color scheme of deep yellows, Tuscan red, beige and olive is particularly beautiful against the soft light of sunrise and sunset, and walking its perimeter along Smokehouse Bay and checking out docked yachts radiating assorted levels of opulence is captivating.

At one stage, there was talk of the city buying the land, but when that didn't materialize, Antaramian forked out the relatively small sum of $1 million to lay claim to it. The subsequent construction of high-end condos atop a 50,000 square-foot waterfront retail center became the perfect example of mixed-use property.

At the same time, and before the infamous real estate bubble peaked in 2006, Antaramian again contributed with a dual high-rise complex called Pier 81, situated on Bald Eagle Drive heading towards Olde Marco. In Olde Marco itself, developers complemented the historic Olde Marco Inn - dating back to 1896 when the son of the island's founder named it the Marco Hotel - with new, low-rise suites.

Residentially, and prior to the bubble, there was plenty of building activity around the island, particularly in the high-end housing area known as "The Estates," in the gated community of Hideaway Beach, and in avenues and cul-de-sacs with spectacular views of the river, Gulf and assorted bays. Razing original Mackle-built homes here and replacing them with larger residences, often built on two original lots, became the

norm. The Mackle brothers, who cut their teeth providing affordable housing for the masses in all of their many Florida communities, including Marco, surely would have seen this coming had they been alive.

RESORT FEVER

Meanwhile, grand hotels were built and refurbished to keep pace with ever-evolving trends.

Best-known is the Marriott, now regarded as one of the jewels in the brand's crown nationally and internationally. It started off humbly enough as the 50-room Marco Beach Hotel in 1965. It then had a facelift, becoming a 100-unit property with villas before major award-winning expansion in 1971. Marriott took over in 1979 having paid $35 million. Further expansion over the years resulted in a second twin tower. Today, the sprawling 727-room guest oasis also features two golf courses, a Balinese spa, ballrooms, restaurants and meeting rooms. Recent upgrades came in at just over $200 million.

Wising up to the island's upscale residential trend at the time, the hotel's new owner, Massachusetts Mutual Financial Group, moved forward with the construction of Madeira, a 17-story luxury tower on the north side of the Marriott property. Prices for units ranged from $1.3 million to more than $5 million. All of the building's 101 units — each owner was required to make a $50,000 deposit — were snapped up before the February 2004 ground-breaking.

Farther south along Collier Boulevard, the Hilton Resort emerged in May 1985. It, too, has undergone numerous multimillion-dollar upgrades including a 10,000 square-foot spa (2008) and a recent $13-million renovation. The resort has 297 rooms, including 29 one-bedroom suites and four luxury, two-bedroom penthouses. The resort prides itself, having won AAA Four Diamond Award rankings in each of the last 14 years.

Between the Marriott and the Hilton on Collier Boulevard is the Marco Beach Ocean Resort, a luxury property affiliated with the off-island Fiddler's Creek development. Opened in 2001, it is the newest resort on Marco.

ABOVE: FROM LEFT, MARRIOTT AND HILTON BEACH VIEWS, RESPECTIVELY

The resort's 100 one- and two-bedroom suites, it has been said, have become a haven for celebrities looking for seclusion.

Additionally, Marriott's Crystal Shores, the island's latest time-share development, was completed in 2008 on the former Radisson Hotel property overlooking the Gulf. A portion of the Radisson's shell was retained in the construction.

THE ISLAND SCENE

Consistent with an expanding island population was that population's desire to intermingle, hence clubs, and more clubs. And plenty more.

Front and center, Sunrise and Noontime Rotary clubs, the Woman's Club, Newcomers Club, Kiwanis Club, American Cancer Society, Civil Air Patrol, Coast Guard Auxiliary, Knights of Columbus and the Italian American Society.

If you're looking for kindred spirits in activities from karate to knitting; books to gardening; chess to Corvettes; Daughters of the American Revolution to the American Association of University Women; nature preservation to sailors and power boaters; boy scouts to an eagle sanctuary foundation; a Moose Lodge to ham radio; Lions (of the two-legged kind) to model yacht enthusiasts; property owners to Shriners, and taxpayers to the local VFW Post 6370, you'll find them all here on this 6 x 4 mile "rock," as Marco is affectionately referred to by locals.

As with any small town, businesses (particularly restaurants) have come and gone, while others have indeed flourished.

Aside from the Olde Marco Inn's storied longevity, only Rose Marina has been in operation here longer. The patriarch was a larger-than-life man by the name of Bill Rose. Pilot, United States Marine, engineer, family man and philanthropist, Rose was a Pennsylvania transplant who arrived in 1956 and passed away in 2010 leaving, as but one legacy, the marina off Bald Eagle Drive on the way to Olde Marco. When it originally

opened in 1969, it carried the name of Marco River Marina, and consisted of a parking lot, small ship's store and a wooden T-shaped dock extending from it. Many of the island's first home buyers sailed in and out of the property.

One enviable trait evident in the veritable national and international mixing pot that is Marco, is philanthropy.

Some examples of that generosity are contributions to organizations like the Joy of Giving (Christmas presents for needy kids, bought by their parents with cash vouchers); Bedtime Bundles (basic necessities for migrant farm worker families just up the road from Marco); The Wounded Warriors Amputee Softball Team; the American Cancer Society; Meals of Hope (for hungry area families, yes, just down the road from Marco), and a wealth of support for at least a dozen organizations that help deserving Marco kids cover some of their college costs by supplying them with scholarships.

FOND GOOD BUYS

One of the most significant city purchases, courtesy of a thumbs-up by its citizens, was the recent purchase of a tract of land for $8 million. Veterans Community Park has since become the outdoor hub for civic and organization gatherings such as the annual Seafood Festival, the weekly Farmer's Market (November to April), Christmas Island Style events such as the tree-lighting ceremony and, of course, Veterans Day and Memorial Day ceremonies.

There was some opposition to the purchase, which came around the time the real estate bubble was about to burst, but it panned out undeniably as a great purchase in the end.

Complementing the "new-look" Marco of the 2000s was the addition of a second span on the Judge S.S. Jolley Bridge. First built as a toll overpass in 1969, it truly opened Marco to the world and helped move home and home site sales considerably at the time. The new addition, built with economic stimulus money at a cost of some $28 million, opened

in mid-2011. It was regarded as a necessity, not only to ensure the island's economic viability, but also from a safety point of view. Here, think hurricanes and evacuations.

The bridge is a subject of great affection for Marco Islanders, who to a person will tell you that they decided to settle here after driving over it and seeing the magnificent view beyond.

The other bridge close to Islanders' hearts is the Goodland Bridge, renamed the Stan Gober Memorial Bridge in January 2013 following his death six months earlier. Residents of the modern era were first introduced to all of Marco's potential glory via a swing bridge. It was the only bridge connecting the mainland to Goodland and Marco via State Road 92. The Jolley span was, at the time, years away. Gober, a local legend as a restaurateur, entertainer and humanitarian from Goodland, created an annual Mullet Festival and accompanying Buzzard Lope song (featuring feathered human females gyrating on stage in madcap style for the coveted Buzzard Queen title). Tens of thousands of grateful revelers of all ages enjoyed the shenanigans for decades.

LEARNING CURVE

With a steadily increasing population, some 17,000 year-round and 40,000 "in season," schools and sports have evolved incrementally as well.

Long-serving Tommie Barfield Elementary was complemented in 1998 by a charter middle school and more recently, in 2010, by a small high school called the Marco Island Academy. The elementary and middle schools have about 450 students each, while the high school started with 60 (freshmen and sophomore) students, and by 2014 had 156 students across all grades. In addition there is the Island Montessori Academy (about 30 students), as well as the private Winterberry Christian Academy (a few students). Pre-schools abound.

Various sports are provided by the middle and high schools and the island is home to The Optimist Club, offering structured youth league sports across the spectrum. For all ages, the city's parks and recreation

ABOVE: FROM LEFT, THE MARCO RIVER, A FAVORITE FISHING SPO FARMER'S MARKET

department has a host of programs often in and around Mackle Park, as does the YMCA at its sprawling facility located at 101 Sandhill Street.

Sundays, some of Marco Island's churches need police help to direct traffic.

There are no shortages of houses to worship here, including: the Family Church of Marco Island (Winterberry Drive), New Life Community Church (W. Elkcam Circle), Marco Presbyterian Church (W. Elkcam Circle), United Church of Marco Island (N. Barfield Drive), San Marco Catholic Church (San Marco Road), Wesley United Methodist Church (S. Barfield Drive), Marco Lutheran Church (N. Collier Blvd.), St. Mark's Episcopal Church (E. Elkcam Circle), and the Jewish Congregation of Marco Island (Winterberry Drive).

Islanders have a host of media options, mostly in print. Three newspapers vie for readers and advertising dollars. The *Marco Island Eagle*, established by retired New York Times' advertising executive William Tamplin in 1968 (now operated by the *Naples Daily News*/Scripps Media, Inc.);

Marco Island Sun Times, established by Tony Lawson, Trecy Tekus and Matt Roseboom in 2001 (now operated by Gannett newspapers); and the monthly *Coastal Breeze News*, established in 2009 by Valerie Simon. The *Sun Times* trio had previously worked for the *Eagle*, and Simon, for the *Sun Times*. Stephen and Debbie Barker, meanwhile, have successfully carved an important niche as publishers of an all-color visitor's guide. *The Marco Review* has been going strong for 20-plus years. Television and radio needs are served by outlets off island although in 2012, after a host of local on-island radio outlets had failed over the years, 98.1 "The Island" debuted. Among a bevy of Marco Island-related websites, marcoislandcommunitytelevision.com adds a video component to many of the happenings here.

HURRICANE PROOF

A quick look at a spaghetti map of hurricanes over the past 80 years reveals that Marco has been hit regularly, just like most of the rest of Florida.

Truth is, Marco has been directly hit by just a single storm, Wilma, in 2005. Earlier, 1960s Donna and the infamous Andrew of 1992 certainly made themselves felt, but Wilma was the one that really got the attention of Marco Islanders. Its eye hit nearby Cape Romano early morning Oct. 24 and it roared across the island as a category 3 storm.

Structural damage, however, was mostly limited to pool cages being demolished while some roof damage was reported. Salt spray devastated plants and shrubs. The back end of the storm was the culprit.

Post-Mackle life on Marco Island has also been highlighted by community interest in its past.

Marco Islanders are by nature fascinated by the history and heritage of the island, and following the formation in 1994 of the Marco Chapter of the Collier County Historical Society, it morphed into the Marco Island Historical Society in 1996.

A one-time small group of concerned residents eventually grew into a 600-member society, and a concerted fundraising effort eventually raised more than $4 million to build the island's gleaming new museum that opened in 2010.

TOP: THE ESPLANADE

OPPOSITE PAGE: SOUTH SEAS TOWERS

PAGES 90 & 91: MARCO'S MAGIC:
WAVE RUNNERS, A MANATEE, DOLPHINS
AND THE INSPIRING TEN THOUSAND
ISLAND CHAIN

CELEBRITY ISLAND

Welcome to Marco Island's Fantasy Celebrity Reunion, a gathering of many of the greats and near-greats who have enjoyed life here over the decades.

The venue for this imaginary reunion is Marco's present-day, very real Veterans Memorial Park. Hosting the gathering is Marco Island's greatest ambassador, golf icon Gene Sarazen. He was one of the first full-time residents of modern Marco Island in the 1960s, due to his friendship with the men who created this place, the Mackle brothers. Another friend of the Mackles, Rev. Billy Graham, blessed today's get-together.

Celebrity residents such as former world heavyweight boxing champion James "Buster" Douglas, who lived here in the early 90s, could hobnob with New York Yankee ace Bob Turley, even though in real life their Marco years were generations apart.

Cartoonist/resident Dale Messick, creator of the Brenda Starr Reporter cartoon series, which ran in 72 major newspapers at its height in 1966, is at her easel, chronicling the arrival of reunion guests.

TV ICONS

At the peel-and-eat shrimp table, next to the long red carpet, we find TV icon Jack Paar, the pioneer talk show host who loved being on Marco so much he did a 1968 promotional film about the island at no charge.

"It's one of Florida's last great islands and one of America's most unspoiled places," Paar said in the promo. "It's not one of those communities of old, retired people. It's a swinging place."

At the party Paar is chatting with some other show biz stars who have come to Marco over the years. He seems instantly taken with TV variety show icon Ed Sullivan and country music star Shania Twain.

Notice the guy with the tan walking up to Shania and Paar? It's actor James Garner. And another fella is approaching them, limping a bit, a bandage on his neck.

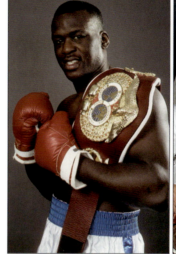

It's super stuntman Evel Knievel. He is praising Marco and suggesting the city build a proper arena for his daredevil antics.

HOLLYWOOD EAST

Sometimes it seems like Hollywood east. Bob Hope is crooning about his love affair with Marco by singing, *"Thanks For The Memories"* to an approving crowd of fellow celebs.

Tom Cruise's mother, Mary Lee South, lived here for years which prompted frequent alleged "sightings" of TC himself. The actor, however, was harder to spot than the green flash at sunset.

This fantasy reunion of people who brought fame (and some fortune) to Marco is rich with musical golden oldies alumni such as Sammy Kaye and trumpeter Harry James and his orchestra, plus stars of almost every decade — Perry Como, Jackie Gleason, Jimmy Dean and Larry Dorr, former manager of Blood Sweat & Tears.

EFT: AN EARLY MORNING DIP
T MARRIOTT

OP RIGHT: TWO OF MARCO'S
MORE PROMINENT CELEBRITIES:
ORMER RESIDENT AND WORLD
EAVYWEIGHT BOXING CHAMPION
AMES "BUSTER" DOUGLAS AND
POLLO 11 ASTRONAUT MICHAEL
OLLINS, SEATED BETWEEN
RST MEN ON THE MOON NEIL
RMSTRONG AND BUZZ ALDRIN

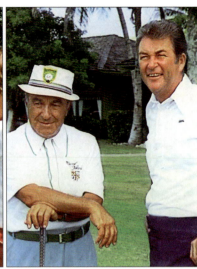

Frank Sinatra came to Marco to get a haircut. Well, he came primarily to visit his friend, golfing great Ken Venturi. But Ol' Blue Eyes needed a trim, so a local hair stylist was summoned. She had the surprise of her life when Sinatra walked in. She says he was a nice guy and a great tipper.

The music makers are gathered in a corner near the bandstand at this outdoor reunion, swapping stories and hairstyles.

That tall guy with the cowboy hat strolling near the fountain is Alan Jackson, who lived on Marco in the 90s. He's strumming his blockbuster hit song, *"Good Time."* Island residents Bill and Karen Young know that while Jackson has moved on, his Washburn Apache acoustic guitar remains in safe hands. When the Youngs bought Jackson's house here, he gave them the guitar with the inscription: "Thanks, Bill, Alan Jackson. Yeehhaw!"

SPORTS SUPERSTARS

We see another crowd forming on the lawn. It seems to be a softball game, chock full of jocks from various eras, all of whom spent time on Marco Island.

It appears that former major league catcher Joe Garagiola, who kept a home here, wanted to pitch, explaining that in his major league career he was not only not the best catcher in baseball, he wasn't even the best catcher on his street growing up. His neighbor in St. Louis was Yogi Berra . . . he, too, visited here.

Billy Martin and Ralph Kiner play rock-paper-scissors to see who gets to bat first.

Joe DiMaggio plays the outfield in this fantasy reunion pickup game. Don Sutton pitches. Mickey Mantle hit two balls into the nearby canal and Roger Maris hit one rocket into the Church of God parking lot.

TOP: LEFT TO RIGHT;
JOE GARAGIOLA;
EVEL KNIEVAL; GENE SAREZEN
WITH KEN VENTURI; ROBERT
MACKLE WITH MICKEY MANTLE

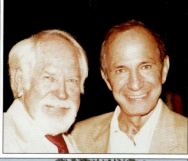
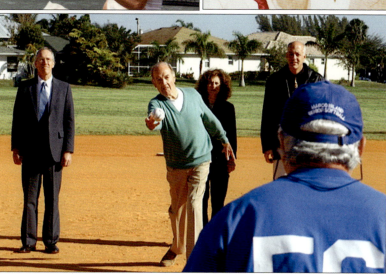

Many of the athletes came to Marco primarily to play in the Tony Lema Memorial Golf Tournament. Lema was the first pro at the Marco Island Country Club (today's Island Country Club) but died in a 1966 plane crash that also took the life of his wife Betty.

The fantasy party was a golf fan's autograph-hunting paradise with big names such as Jack Nicklaus, Tom Watson, Ben Crenshaw and, of course, Marco's first celebrity to call it home: Sarazen hosting the Lema festivities each year.

Some of the pros opted for the nearby putt-putt course, just to make it fair. That included stars of other big league sports, who fancied themselves secret golf pros too.

Who knew that former Notre Dame football coach Ara Parseghian would be an early homeowner here? Other grid-iron greats, Dave Kocourek, Mike Vanderjagt and Dan Dierdorf have lived here while George Blanda, Terry Bradshaw, coach Don Shula and "Broadway Joe" Namath also enjoyed Marco's spoils as participants in the Lema tournament.

SOAP STARS

Two long-running festivals livened up the island over the years, bringing once and future stars of Hollywood and television here.

In 1998, a handful of imaginative locals created the Marco Island Film Festival, in hopes such an annual event would bring tourists to help island businesses turn summer doldrums into dollars.

The film event brought interesting movies and some big-name stars as well, including the sex symbol superstar of the 40s and 50s, Jane Russell.

She is spotted standing under a mahogany tree, chatting with Jane Seymour and Gwen Verdon.

A few years after the film festival began, Marco's "Soapfest" sprang to life, a favorite annual gathering of scores of soap opera stars, attended by adoring, addicted soap fans from far and wide.

Some made it to this fantasy reunion too. Walt Willy loves Marco as much as his fans have loved him. He played Jackson Montgomery on the soap "All My Children" for 24 years.

By the Tang concession stand, we spot astronauts Michael Collins, Gene Cernan and Jack Swigert.

Collins, who has lived quietly on Marco in retirement, was the command module pilot for Apollo 11. He orbited the moon in July 1969 while astronauts Neil Armstrong and Buzz Aldrin made the first manned landing on the lunar surface. It may very well have been mankind's greatest achievement.

STAR SPANGLED CELEBS

This fantasy reunion also has some star-spangled celebs from other walks of life.

The great TV news anchorman, Howard K. Smith, moved into a beach front condo near the end of his stellar career. At this party, he talks quietly with a famous Marco Islander, former war hero and presidential candidate George McGovern.

McGovern had been asked to throw out the first pitch at the season opener of the Marco Seniors Softball League game back in 2004 and is telling Smith all about it.

Meanwhile, a free-throw or two away, NBA great Bill Laimbeer, former NBA coach Allan Bristow, tennis titan Martina Navratilova and LPGA Hall of Famer Pat Bradley are comparing style points. Nearby, other big shots are swapping state secrets. Or photos of the grandkids.

One is John Boehner, the Republican Speaker of the House. He's the very latest in a long line of power brokers and celebrities to call this place home.

Syndicated radio talk show host Neal Boortz, once a Marco homeowner, enjoyed an exclusive sit-down interview with Boehner.

Presidents have come to Marco, too, including Richard Nixon and Gerald Ford and both made cameo appearances at this fantasy reunion, as does Ford's wife Betty.

A clutch of ladies sip cosmos at the bar, but morph into a gaggle of autograph seekers when they see a tall, handsome man talking with Marco restaurateur Judy Barney. He is Salvatore Ferragamo, as in Ferragamo shoe fame.

The female fans calm a bit when they realized that Ferragamo spends more time on the family wine business than on designer footwear.

Banker and part-time resident John Lauritzen keeps a close eye on the reunion's bar and food tab. Lauritzen, who became America's youngest bank president at the age of 29 when he purchased Emerson State Bank

TOP: LEFT TO RIGHT;
ROGER LOGGIA, JANE RUSSELL
AND DEAN STOCKWELL;
MARIO LOPEZ; BRITTANY SNOW
AND PATRICIA BERRY

in Iowa, would later pioneer the charge card concept having introduced First National Bank of Omaha's first charge card. Visa and MasterCard would soon follow.

Meanwhile, cleaning giant and Marco resident Stanley Steemer eyes the reunion's already worn red carpet. It would no doubt need cleaning. Rising young Hollywood actress Leighton Meester, who lived here briefly, assures fans she will indeed be back on the good-as-new red carpet for next year's reunion.

MARCO'S MAGICAL ESSENCE

"Where are we going?" Wendy asked from her drafty window perch as she overlooked the snowy rooftops of old London town.

"Well it's simple," Peter Pan replied. "We're going to the most wonderful place ever. It's an island paradise where it never gets cold, where wonderful sea creatures and mermaids swim in the water and it's an ancient and magical island where a tribe of Indians once lived and absolutely anything is possible. It's called Never Neverland and all we have to do is steer for the second star on the right and go straight on till morning."

Of course, everyone knows the story of Peter Pan is only a fairy tale. It was created to amuse and delight, to entertain and to inspire, and to bridge the world of reality into a private world of fantasy that only the young at heart can hold in a very special place for the rest of their lives.

TRANSPORTING THE SENSES

If a Never Neverland truly exists it must be located here on Marco Island.

For almost everyone, and especially those who are and will always be very young at heart, topping the rise over the bridge to Marco will amuse and delight, entertain and inspire. When the magic of Marco Island begins to emerge and casts her charm, visitors and islanders alike will keep their course steady and straight, to return again and again, to the shining star that continues to enchant generations from around the globe.

Imagine a tropical island tucked away and nestled into one of the largest mangrove forests in the world. Now imagine a vast archipelago of Ten Thousand Islands reaching out and surrounding this magical island with water the color of emeralds, with sandy beaches the color of sugar, and lush tropical palms and endless flowering foliage. This special place transports the senses to everything Polynesian and the wistful reminiscence of the legends of the South Seas.

In autumn and winter the clear skies over Marco silhouette coconut palms in a sailor's favorite sunset, but as spring grows into summer,

towering columns of sun-touched clouds can turn into nightly fireworks as rainbows give way to thundershowers over the Gulf. The discharge of lightning hosts an endless display of illumination that can only be described as extraordinary and unbelievable.

Every season has a charm and the subtle change of seasons always leads to debate. Newcomers will undoubtedly hail winter and spring as the favorite months but veterans of island living will often claim the Caribbean-like summers on Marco are the absolute favorite. In winter or summer there is always a breeze and if the tropical weather of June, July, and August becomes too much, thundershowers flourish over the archipelago and, as the island cools, every flower imaginable blooms and colors the landscape.

Centuries ago, Calusa Indians enjoyed the changing seasons of Marco and revered them as much as the overflowing artesian springs that produced a bountiful supply of fresh water. Add fish teeming in the local waters, and the culture thrived in the only subtropical zone in America other than the Hawaiian Islands.

CHARMING GENERATIONS

Long after the Calusa, early settlers and pioneers laid claim to the land, establishing a trading post and a hotel in Marco village to the north. Within a century of the island's 1870 founding, a modern Marco Island would emerge to cast her charm. Over the last 50 years, a casual elegance has evolved that attracts a very special type of resident and returning visitor.

Today, Marco Island is unique as it gets and very different from its neighbors. It is also home to burrowing owl habitats. These wise and sage little creatures that choose to live here are not found in Naples or even south in Everglades City. They are not found in Miami, Fort Lauderdale, or even Palm Beach. They are a very reserved and intelligent species that legend has always held high as an example of practical patience and down-to-earth common sense. The burrowing owls of Marco seem to emulate their human Marco Island neighbors. They do not preen to the point of being pretentious and they do not call attention to themselves with ostentatious overbearing.

Recently, at a South Florida retirement party for a veteran banker of 40 years, a question was asked about the difference between Marco and other communities in the region.

"Marco is very different," the well-seasoned banker began. "Marco is like no other place. In Miami, Palm Beach or even Naples, people will leverage their money so they can drive a Bentley, a Ferrari, or even a Rolls Royce. They do this so they can drive and pull up at a prominent restaurant so everyone can see them. Then they pause beside their perfectly polished car so everyone can have a good look. Afterward they parade into the eatery and toss their Ferrari car keys down so even the restaurant staff will know how wealthy and special they are."

The veteran banker then paused with a smile. "But the folks on Marco are totally different — and I've seen their bank accounts. They have just as much money as the people with the fancy cars but they drive 10-year-old Fords. That's the difference between most places and Marco. Marco people are private, patient, and very polished, but they just aren't the type to show off."

MARCO SECRETS

Apart from the diversity of the island inhabitants and the special allure that the magic of Marco does cast, visitors and residents are drawn to a modern and real Never Neverland for many reasons that are not common knowledge.

Marco Island has one of the lowest crime rates in the State of Florida. It has no urban air-pollution and some of the most oxygen-rich and freshest air in the nation. As everyone continues to visit and explore the Marco-brand of an island paradise that truly is a fable brought to life, there is a consistent observation made by those who have just arrived.

"Everything is so clean and everyone is so nice," the first-time visitors invariably exclaim.

Marco is closer to Cuba and the Caribbean Sea than it is to Tampa and because of the shallow warm waters of the Gulf and the nutrient rich eco-

TOP: THE JOY OF ISLAND LIVING

system provided by the surrounding mangroves, the delicate magic of Marco reaches out to provide some of the finest fishing ever.

When shallow water anglers from around the world cross the Judge S. S. Jolley Bridge and look out across the endless mangroves and the Marco River, visions of pulling in trophy-sized snook, redfish or tarpon whets the appetite and inspires the imagination. Offshore, deepwater scuba divers and salt-water anglers are drawn to the mystery and adventure that waits just beyond the horizon and easily envision old shipwrecks swarming with sea turtles and multitudes of tropical fish. The numerous shipwrecks that lie unforgotten and waiting offshore are a continuing testament to lost tragedies of World War II and a time when global aggressions touched the edge of paradise.

There are over 100 golf courses between Marco and Fort Myers and a holiday spent on Marco can easily encompass enough golf to handicap even the most steadfast enthusiast. Meanwhile, a sailing trip to a nearby sandbar can provide enough collectable seashells to satisfy the souvenir needs of anyone searching for a perfect island keepsake.

THE AMERICAN DREAM

The story of modern Marco Island began in 1962 when three brothers walked our deserted, crescent-shaped beach for the very first time. Marco at the time was really a series of mangrove islands surrounded by a spectacular crescent-shaped beach, but the vision of a tropical resort/leisure community that would rival any destination in the world became a reality only because of the tenacious resolve of three brothers that shared the name Mackle.

Elliott, Robert and Frank Jr. lovingly created, reclaimed and nurtured Marco Island. They created a playground like no other. A modern day fairy tale to amuse and delight, to entertain and to inspire, and to bridge the world of reality into a very special community that remains to this day a true testament to the power of the American dream.

During the days of the Spanish Main, when Henry Morgan reigned supreme in Jamaica and pirates set sail for plunder, the conquistadors arrived on Marco Island and believed they found the fountain of youth. Island residents and visitors today can find validation in the early explorers' beliefs as they look to *National Geographic* magazine and discover that Collier County (where Marco Island sits) is listed as the number one region in North America for longevity and continuing good health. TripAdvisor online readers recently listed Marco Island as the No. 1 island travel destination in America and fourth best in the world.

No wonder. With every year, every season, and every single day, the magic, the charm, and casual elegance of Marco Island continues to evolve and will always attract visitors and islanders alike to return again and again — to a very special shining star that continues to enchant generations from around the globe.

THE WRITERS & PHOTOGRAPHERS

MICHAEL COLEMAN

His endless wanderlust has taken him to over 100 of the world's most fascinating countries but it is here on Marco Island where he feels most at home. Hailing from a newspaper and television news background, Michael parlayed his media experience to become Press Secretary to Canada's Minister of Tourism, an Executive Editor at the *Marco Island Eagle*, and Cruise Travel Columnist at the *Marco Island Sun Times*. He authored his first book, *Marco Island Culture & History*, in 1995. The seeds for *Marco Island, Florida's Gulf Playground*, in celebration of the modern era's 50th birthday in 2015, were sewn a couple of years ago as he flipped through the pages of an inspiring history publication at a bookstore a world away from Marco in, of all places, Dubai. The city was celebrating the 40th birthday of its modern era.

marcohistory@hotmail.com   www.marcoislandbook.com

DON FARMER & CHRIS CURLE

Dynamic husband and wife duo, Don and Chris have covered heroes and villains, rogues and rock stars, presidents and potentates around the world during their combined nine decades of working at major television news outlets. When CNN debuted on June 1, 1980, Don and Chris were front and center among the fledgling startup's first anchors. In those busy years, the couple came to Marco Island at every opportunity, planning all the while to live here full time one day. That day came in 1997. Much of the action in their new novel, *Deadly News*, happens in and around Marco Island. Don also co-authored *Roomies: Tales From the Worlds of TV News and Sports*, a book he wrote with his college roommate and lifelong friend, the late, legendary sportscaster, Skip Caray.

donfarmer@me.com   chris@chriscurle.com   www.deadlynewsthriller.com

JOEL GEWIRTZ

Although Joel is a highly regarded CPA and prolific local volunteer, photography is his true passion. He has been taking images for as long as he can remember and, a decade ago, he captured much of Marco Island's beauty by publishing his own hardcover photographic book. Pending retirement does not mean that Joel will sit still. He is now setting his sights on publishing a series of photo books. A New York City native, he has lived on Marco Island for over 30 years. He started the island's first Kiwanis Club in 1994; was named Marco's Volunteer of the Year that same year; and, among a host of other local causes and contributions, he has been a member of both Leadership Marco and Leadership Collier programs.

walkmarco@aol.com

BARRY HOWE

Whether shooting aerials or setting up for a timed exposure cityscape, Howe has a most discerning eye behind the lens. A Duke University graduate and Vietnam veteran, he began a commercial photography business in Marina Del Rey, California, in 1973. He has since photographed national parks and exotic landscapes but is perhaps best known for his inspiring aerial photographs of stadiums and ballparks across America. In 2001, he first turned his lens on Marco Island. Most of his city photomurals were taken with a Dierdorff 8 x 10 view camera and his aerials with a medium format camera. In a digital age he continues to shoot with film and, among Barry's photos in this book, are the stunning front and back covers featuring our island like it has never been captured before.

barry@barryhowe.com   barryhowephotography@comcast.net   www.barryhowe.com

MARION NICOLAY

A self-described "army brat," Marion has lived all over the country and in foreign lands. In college she engaged in amateur theater. Along the way she earned a bachelor's degree in science and an MA in art education. Career stints included that of a sales girl, secretary, journalist, high school art teacher and private pilot. A founding member of the Marco Island Historical Society, she returned to her love of theater as a history re-enactor portraying Deaconess Harriet Bedell, Nancy Reagan and Pat Nixon over the years. For almost a quarter of a century, her food and history newspaper columns appeared weekly in the *Marco Island Eagle* and later in the *Marco Island Sun Times*. Just recently she won a coveted award for her history writing.

marion387@centurylink.net

ELIZABETH "BETSY" PERDICHIZZI

A prolific writer about Marco's history, Betsy first fell in love with the island in 1989. She has since written four books: *A Girl Called Tommie, Queen of Marco Island; The Phony Hermit; Into the Florida Wilderness, A Journey with Drs. Mary and Louis Olds;* and *Island Voices, They Came to Marco Island.* She was instrumental in establishing the Marco Island Historical Society and equally pivotal in the capital campaign to raise $4.5 million dollars to build the Marco Island Historical Museum. She served two terms as chairman of the Collier County Historical Preservation Board. She was named Marco Island Citizen of the Year; received the Spirit of Marco Island award by the Rotary Clubs of America; and the Golden Quill, a journalism award presented by the Florida Historical Society for excellence in writing.

betsyperd@comcast.net   www.caxambaspublishing.com   www.amazon.com/author/betsyperdichizzi

QUENTIN ROUX

A full-time, award-winning writer and photographer on Marco Island for almost two decades, Roux began his professional career as a magazine journalist and assistant editor for 18 years based in Durban, South Africa. He is the go-to veteran writer, photographer and videographer for the *Marco Island Sun Times*, which he describes as the island's "progressive" publication. He has won a host of state press awards during his tenure, including first place honors for feature photography, criticism (movie) writing, feature, business, humorous and serious column writing. Like most residents before him, he fell in love with Marco Island the minute he first arrived. Roux says he became passionate about community journalism when learning that Marco residents were so appreciative of local news coverage.

qroux@yahoo.com   www.marcoislandforida.com

TOM WILLIAMS

His love affair with writing culminated in 2014 when his latest novel, a non-fiction historical narrative about the golden age of the American space program, earned top honors in the Florida Book Awards non-fiction category. *Surrounded by Thunder - The Story of Darrell Loan and the Rocket Men* reads like an adventure novel, but the characters, the timeline, and all the incredible achievements of the early days of space exploration are true. His first novel, *Lost and Found* was published in 2008 and was ranked among the top five books "to must take on vacation" by *Sport Diver* magazine in 2013. Tom is celebrating his 35th year as an employee at the Marco Island Marriott Beach Resort, Golf Club & Spa where, as captain, he takes guests on spectacular sailing and shelling tours into the Ten Thousand Islands.

capttom@marcoislandtoday.com

BIBLIOGRAPHY

Anderson, Ray, Interviews with author, 1995

Archives/Publications: *American Builder* magazine; *Chicago Tribune; Coastal Breeze News; Collier County News;* Deltona corporate documents, various annual reports, sales brochures, newspaper supplements, advertisements and other company promotional materials including *The Marco Islander* newsletter; *Forbes* magazine; *Fort Myers News-Press; Fort Myers Press; Lakeland Ledger;* Mackle III, Frank, family archives; Marco Island Area Chamber of Commerce visitor guides, *Marco Island Eagle; Marco Island Sun Times; Miami Herald; The Miami News;* murderpedia.org; *Naples Daily News; Naples Sun;* NASA media archives; *National Geographic* magazine; Reuters news agency; *St. Petersburg Times; The New York Times; Time* magazine.

Bahr, Neil, Interviews with author, 2009, 2005, 1995

Beater, Jack, *Tales of South Florida and the Ten Thousand Islands,* Ace Press, C 1965, Fort Myers, FL

Beckhorn, Ed, Interviews with author, 1995

Biles, Fay, Interviews with author, 1995

Blanchard, Frank, Interviews with author, 1995

Blomeier, Marion, Interviews with author, 1995

Boyer, Howard & Cindy, Interviews with author, 1995

Bruno, Betty, Interviews with author, 1995

Camacho, Steve, Interviews with author, 1995

Canady, Debbie, Interviews with author, 1995

Coleman, Michael, *Marco Island Culture & History,* Marco Island Area Chamber of Commerce, C 1995

Curle, Chris, Interviews with author, 2014, 2013

Dauray, Charles, Interviews with author, 1995

Day, Ed, Interviews with author, 1995

Farmer, Don, Interviews with author, 2014, 2013

Florida: From Indian Trail to Space Age, The Southern Publishing Company, C 1965, Delray Beach, FL

Gardner, Mary, Interviews with author, 1995

Gilliland, Marion, *Key Marco's Buried Treasure,* University of Florida Press, C 1989, Gainesville, FL

Gilliland, Marion, *The Material Culture of Key Marco* Florida, University Presses of Florida, C 1975, Gainesville, FL

Heath, Thelma, Interviews with author, 1995

Hunt, Kathy, Interviews with author, 2014, 2013, 1995

Jamro, Ron, Interviews with author, 1995

Kirk, Bud, Interviews with author, 1995

Kirk, Kappy, Interviews with author, 2005, 1995

Library, Marco Island, Various periodicals, files, resource & reference materials

Llewellyn, Leonard, Interviews with author, 1995

Mackle III, Frank, Interviews with author, 2014, 2013, 2007, 2005

Middlebrook, Chris, Interviews with author, 1995

Museum, Collier County, Various periodicals, files, resource & reference materials

Museum, Marco Island Historical, Various periodicals, files, resource & reference materials

Neale, Pat & Mary, Interviews with author, 1995

Needles, Marv, Interviews with author, 1995

Nicolay, Marion, Interviews with author, 2014, 2013, 2005, 1995

Nordell, Gil, Interviews with author 2008, 2007, 2005

Oyer, Steve, Interviews with author, 1995

Parlipiano, Sil, Interviews with author, 1995

Perdichizzi, Bill, Interviews with author, 2014, 2013, 2005

Perdichizzi, Elizabeth "Betsy", Interviews with author, 2014, 2013, 2005, 1995

Perdichizzi, Elizabeth "Betsy", *A Girl Called Tommie, Queen of Marco Island,* Caxambas Publishing, C 1999

Perdichizzi, Elizabeth "Betsy", *Island Voices, They Came To Marco Island,* Caxambas Publishing, C 2006

Perdichizzi, Elizabeth "Betsy", *Into The Florida Wilderness, A Journey with Drs. Mary and Louis Olds,* Caxambas Publishing, C 2013

Quesnell, Quentin, Interviews with author, 1995

Rimes, Marilyn, Interviews with author, 1995

Roux, Quentin, Interviews with author, 2014, 2013

Sarazen, Gene, Interviews with author, 1995, 1994

Savage, Herb, Interviews with author, 2014, 2013, 2010, 2009, 2005, 1995

Shanahan, Dick & Cathy, Interviews with author, 1995

Stackpoole, James, Interviews with author, 2005

Stone, Maria, *The Caxambas Kid,* Stone Enterprises, C 1987, Naples, FL

Stone, Maria, *The Caxambas Kid II,* Stone Enterprises, C 1989, Naples, FL

Tebeau, Charlton W., *Florida's Last Frontier,* University of Miami Press, C 1957 and 1966

Tenney, Frank, Interviews with author, 1995

Vann, Harold, Interviews with author, 1995

Waitley, Douglas, *The Last Paradise, The Building of Marco Island,* Pickering Press, C 1993, Coconut Grove, FL

Weeks, Cecelia, Interviews with author, 1995

Widmer, Randolph J., Interviews with author, 1995

Widmer, Randolph J., *The Evolution of the Calusa,* University of Alabama Press, C 1988

Williams, Tom, Interviews with author, 2014, 2013

Woodward, Art & Glenellen, Interviews with author, 1995